Cyberpower for Business

By
Wally Bock and Jeff Senné

CAREER PRESS
3 Tice Road
P.O. Box 687
Franklin Lakes, NJ 07417
1-800-CAREER-1
201-848-0310 (NJ and outside U.S.)
FAX: 201-848-1727

CYBERPOWER FOR BUSINESS
ISBN 1-56414-226-4, $14.99
Cover design by Dean Johnson Design, Inc.
Printed in the U.S.A. by Book-mart Press

To order this title by mail, please include price as noted above, $2.50 handling per order, and $1.00 for each book ordered. Send to: Career Press, Inc., 3 Tice Road, P.O. Box 687, Franklin Lakes, NJ 07417.

Or call toll-free 1-800-CAREER-1 (NJ and Canada: 201-848-0310) to order using VISA or MasterCard, or for further information on books from Career Press.

Library of Congress Cataloging-in-Publication Data

Bock, Wally, 1946 -
 Cyberpower for business / by Walter H. Bock and Jeff Senné.
  p. cm.
 Includes index.
 ISBN 1-56414-226-4 (pbk.)
  1. Internet marketing. 2. Business enterprises--Computer networks. 3. Internet marketing. 4. Customer service. 5. Internet advertising. 6. Business--Research. 7. Internet (Computer network) 8. World Wide Web (Information retrieval system) I. Senné, Jeffrey N. II. Title.
 HF5415.1265.B63   1996
 658.8'00285'467--dc20   95-52807
                                                             CIP

658.4
B665

Dedication

To my grandson Teddy, who had his own Web page when he was hours old, received newspapers from friends around the world who were alerted to his birth by e-mail and who will grow up thinking all this is routine.

—Wally Bock

I dedicate this book to my friend, life partner and professional colleague Michelle Murphy. Together we share a special vision that the business community can use the World Wide Web to increase productive communication, prosper and enhance the quality of life we all share in our "global village" as we move into the 21st century in style.

—Jeff Senné

Acknowledgments

We want to start by thanking those who are close to us. For Wally, it's family and the myriad of folks that show up and live with us from time to time. For Jeff, it's his special friend Michelle Murphy and his two sons, Jared and Justin, who are still wondering how and why their father turned into a computer nerd when he turned 40.

We are both active in the National Speakers Association, so we'd like to thank our friends and colleagues from there.

For Wally, there needs to be special mention of Dan Burrus and Patricia Fripp who provide help, encouragement and inspiration at what seems just the right time. For Jeff, it's also Patricia Fripp for her inspiration, Jeff Herman for being our literary agent and getting this book published, Jim and Naomi Rhode for their faith and prayers.

Then there are all the folks that let us work with them: our audiences and clients. We've learned from them.

Wally would like to send special thanks to Tom Vassos of IBM. His knowledge is extensive and his skill is formidable—and his willingness to share both is a model for all of us. He would also like to thank Dan Janal. Our short conversations always take longer than we thought and we don't have lunch often enough. Also, special mention for an absent friend, Tom Mandel, SRI Futurist and online buddy until his untimely death.

Jeff's special mention is for Willis Harman and all of his international business friends from the World Business Academy. And his partner and Webmaster, Ken Braly, for the many hours he has put into making their Web site, The Expertise Center, a true cyber community for their many business clients.

Finally, we'd like to thank our heroes. For Wally that would include John von Neumann and Richard Feynman, George Marshall and Peter Drucker and Enrico Caruso. For Jeff, it is Albert Schweitzer. We used you as models and inspiration and someday, when we grow up, we want to be as good at what we do as you are and were at what you do.

Foreword

Back in the mid 1980s, I identified "distributive computing" as one of the 20 core technologies that would drive permanent change and shape the future. When I wrote *Technotrends* (HarperBusiness) in 1993, the Internet, as we now know it, was just a blip on most business radar screens, the most sprawling example of distributive computing, accessed mostly by scientists, scholarly researchers and computer hackers.

How different things are today!

It's almost impossible to read a book or pick up a magazine without hearing about the Internet and the World Wide Web.

My local bookstore's Internet section has gone from a couple of books to almost a third of the store. Internet business consultants are sprouting like weeds after a spring rain.

The Internet and the World Wide Web are part of the major shifts in focus that I spoke about in *Technotrends*. There I dealt with the need for businesses to shift from concentrating on access to capital to concentrating on access to information. I cited the importance of shifting from thinking global to *being* global, and from focusing on an internal market to focusing on a global market. Many other trends, toward innovation, shorter cycle times, and decentralized communication, are all feeding on or are fostered by the Internet and World Wide Web.

In my own life and business, we at Burrus Research Associates, Inc., make extensive use of electronic mail to communicate. Our Web site (http://www.burrus.com) is one of the ways we get the word out about what we do, as well as sell our products and help our clients. Actually, it's that last item—"help our clients"—that's most exciting. The Internet and the Web give us the capability to form close and enduring links with our clients, and as a result, our clients will be helping us as we help them.

I cannot possibly overemphasize this feature of the Internet. As an author, speaker, science forecaster and strategic consultant to top corporations I harp—yes, harp—on the need to network with all. And I mean *all*. Not just all the members of the team, the division or the company itself. We're talking macro here—*mega* macro! Technology makes it possible to, in a paraphrase of the old AT&T long distance ad, reach out and touch almost *everybody*. Through the Internet and Web, you can link up with your suppliers, distributors, resellers, customers, the customers' customers, and the customers' customers' prospective customers.

Thanks to the Internet we are moving from an emphasis on the marketplace to concentrating on *marketspace*. I call it the zone of maximum value.

The Internet facilitates the formation of a myriad of virtual communities with a two-way flow of time-shifted communication. Precious real-time can be reserved and carefully managed to control cost. In addition, it is multi-dimensional communication. What an ideal collaborative tool! Used this way, the Internet and Web will help move companies out of the Information Age, which is burying us all under an avalanche of data, into the Communication Age, where value is created by extracting and *sharing* actionable knowledge. The benefits go far beyond simply selling a product or a service.

Indeed, networking with all is a powerful practical strategic application made possible by the Internet and the Web. And the full range of strategies that I presented in *Technotrends* can be implemented with dramatic results via similar practical applications as well.

There's just one problem: Most of what's been written about the Internet and the World Wide Web hasn't focused on practical applications. The bulk of what I've seen, heard, and read has concentrated on the Internet and the Web themselves, not on how they're going to be used in businesses today and tomorrow. Until now.

Wally Bock and Jeff Senné have written an excellent handbook for business people and for anyone who intends to spend the rest of his or her life in the rapidly changing place known as "the future." This book provides an abundance of practical applications, but it's more than that. It focuses on strategy, which must be management's highest priority in the years ahead.

Some people fear the Internet as a threat to traditional markets and ways of doing business. If you're one of the skeptics, you've come to the right authors. They see the Internet as an historic opportunity.

I agree totally.

As we in business move from local to global markets, and from focusing on process to focusing on strategy, this book will become ever more important. It has real shelf-life. There's nothing perishable in here about "surfing" or about the latest neat, new Internet technologies of the moment.

Instead, *Cyberpower for Business* will give you the strategic tools you need to position yourself and your business for success in the 21st century. Wally Bock and Jeff Senné have taken their practical experience as speakers, writers, consultants and business executives and poured it into this book. Reading it will save you time and money and get you on the road to success.

As an investment in actionable knowledge, it is totally blue-chip and red-hot—a well-written book by techno-savvy business people that's loaded with strategic business tools. I encourage you and every key executive in your company and industry to read it—and put it to work.

—Daniel Burrus, leading technology
forecaster and author of *Technotrends*

Contents

Preface

Why should you buy this book? Because you are in business and want to be on top of the technology that's changing the way business is done. Because you want to know the proven strategies for succeeding in the new, transformed world. Because it will help you and your business make money faster, more productively and with greater ease.

This book is not about technology! That is to say, in this book we have intentionally stayed away from the technical aspects of the World Wide Web and the Internet and emphasized the practical business possibilities in order to stir your imagination of how you can use this powerful technological medium in your business activities to do things faster, less expensively and more productively. We believe the Internet is no more than a technological tool, albeit a very powerful tool, that when used by everyday business people will enable them to maximize the potential of their commercial endeavors to serve their marketplace.

Results! That's what today's executives are looking for—faster, more accurate, enduring results. Yet in this world where the rules of the game and the market forces change constantly, results are harder than ever to achieve.

In the race for survival, business leaders must meet the challenges and needs of both their newly empowered information employees and their ever demanding customers.

Basically this is a business book written for the everyday business person by a couple guys who first have made their living owning and operating their own businesses for the last 30 years or so producing those kind of results for ourselves and our many clients. For more than a decade we have found that we could use the technology of the Internet and the World Wide Web as powerful business tools to produce faster, more accurate and enduring results for ourselves and our clients. We believe that this business perspective is missing in the many books on the marketplace today about the World Wide Web and the Internet.

This book is written for the business person who may not be technically inclined but who wishes to make use of the World Wide Web and the Internet to enhance business endeavors well into the 21st century. As one of our many seminar attendees said in a recent programs, "I found it refreshing to find an instructor around my own age presenting rather than some wet-behind-the-ears kid guru who doesn't have the slightest consideration for where we have been nor how we got here. Just a personal plus.... I think that perspective added much to your presentation."

In order to stay on course with our unique perspective and to aid you in reading this book we have included an extensive glossary of the many new terms that make up the vocabulary of the World Wide Web and the Internet. Additionally, we have listed each chapter's key points at the beginning to allow you to skim for key information or guide your reading. At the end of each chapter when we cover a particular business function, we have included a list of the applications you can make with the Internet and World Wide Web tools covered throughout the book in order to enable you to make immediate practical use of these tools in your business.

It does not matter if you are technically inclined in order for you to make use of this new technological medium. You will find that there are always people around who can help you with the technical issues. Your job, as a business person, is to see how the Internet tools, techniques, sites and ideas apply to your overall business purpose. It is your primary job to see how they fit into your overall business strategy.

We have found that it is inherent in the nature and makeup of a business person that once the imagination is stirred, a drive for action and results will set a thing in motion. As you move through this book, your challenge is to connect your business experience and what you know about your business activities with what you are learning about the exciting online world of the World Wide Web and the Internet. In doing so, you will be able to make practical use of this technological medium and integrate it into your everyday business practices. And then as the translator, the person standing between the purely business people on one side and the technological people on the other side, it will be time for you to take the step every pioneer has made and lead your business into building its presence on the Web and or the Internet.

You will find that by using the Internet and the World Wide Web in your everyday business communications, you will begin to experience *Cyberpower*, the power of information and connection. Cyberpower provides information when you need it, in forms that you can use. Cyberpower provides connections with people, people in every part of the globe and with every imaginable variation of interest, expertise and need. Cyberpower provides business, buying and selling.

Businesses are only just now discovering the power of this tool that transforms organizations and relationships. This book is about that transformation. It's about powerful tools and exciting opportunity. Because Cyberpower transforms the businesses it touches, this book is about catching a great wave of change.

Cyberpower presents the opportunity for someone out there to become the next Henry Ford. That means that it presents the opportunity to become phenomenally successful in business. But it also presents the opportunity to have your own encyclopedia entry. This book is about Cyberpower and that opportunity.

Many business leaders are frustrated and confused because the "old ways" do not work in the new business environment of the Information Revolution. Old-style business structure is based on paper flow, traditional jobs and traditional boundaries between the organization and the "outside." It is based on control from the top-down and obedience from the bottom-up because people at the top of the pyramid have more information than those at the bottom. It is based on the idea that marketing and sales are things that you do to others, rather than with them. And it worked. Until recently.

But now the trends in the news make it obvious that we are standing on the crest of a wave that will revolutionize the way we do business forever. Everywhere you turn, you see and hear the buzz and blur of articles on businesses reengineering processes through information technology.

It's obvious that there's a big change going on. And it's more than just a change in technology. It's more than the Internet. It's more than the creation of new markets and ordering pizza from your computer. But there's almost no practical information about what all these changes really mean for business and how a business executive can profit from them.

We wrote this book to help fill the information void this technological change is creating in our increasingly networked global marketplace. *Cyberpower for Business* isn't just another book on networking or the technical aspects of how the software and infrastructure works. *Cyberpower for Business* is for the practical everyday business person who wants to know what profitable results can be produced and how to make use of this powerful strategic tool called the Internet.

Chapter 1

Transforming Technologies

Key points

- We're in the midst of a vast transformation of the way we do business, and two of the engines powering that change are the Internet and the World Wide Web.

- One way to understand how individuals and businesses are adopting and using the Internet and World Wide Web is to look at the way they adopted and used television when it became popular.

- In the beginning of TV, we only had old business models to adapt to it, but we learned fast.

- The next eight to 10 years will be a period of growth and learning about how to do business on the Net/Web.

- In 1989 there were only 600,000 people on the Net. Today there are as many as 75 million.

- Innovations in the last five years have made the Net/Web easier to use. That will continue.

- This revolution and growth will happen with you or without you.

Cyberpower for Business

• Doing business in Cyberspace is getting easier and more profitable, and this book will show you how.

It's made the cover of *Time* magazine. More than once. It fills conversations on commuter trains and airplanes and at parties and business luncheons. It even has its own aspect of business snobbery, "Oh, you don't have e-mail?" It's the Internet and the World Wide Web.

In recent months we've seen an explosion of materials about doing business in cyberspace. The possibilities are exciting—even more exciting than you've experienced so far. We're in the midst of a vast transformation in the way we do business, and one of the engines powering that change is the communication technology that can immediately connect us with virtually anyone in the world. And we're just now entering the high-growth phase of these particular tools.

This book is about doing business on the Internet and the World Wide Web. It's about how you can use exciting new communication technologies to perform business functions you already know—but enhance them, do them better, and do them more profitably.

But before we get to our strategies, tools, business models and specific techniques, we need to step back for a second and give you an idea of just how dramatic this change is and how it might relate to your business.

The best analogy for the kind of change we're undergoing right now is the introduction of television as a commercial medium.

The first commercial demonstration of television was conducted by a British inventor named J. L. Baird in 1926, and the first commercial broadcast occurred in the 30s. After a short break for World War II, strong effort resumed to expand television and its commercial possibilities. But television didn't take right away.

No, the development of television, like most other technological innovations, followed a pretty standard development model called the S Curve. Essentially, the S Curve shows that for an initial period of time, growth is very slow—after which there is an explosion of growth. Then the growth curve flattens out again. That's what happened with television.

Television sales grew steadily after World War II, but not at a tremendous rate. The first year of significant growth was 1953: television sales took off and kept rising through the early part of the 1960s. During that time, television had a transforming impact on American life.

That's about where things are with the Net right now. While it's been around for quite a while, but we've just gone into the growth phase in the last year. Every week 10,000 new accounts are opened with commercial online gateways. More than 1,200 new Web sites are added to the World Wide Web every day. And in the first nine months of 1995, the number of commercial domains jumped from 29,000 to 114,000.

The Net has just entered its high growth phase. So what can we learn from going back to the adoption of television? Let's let one of our authors tell this one in the first person.

"We got our first television set in 1953. I was a kid. We got it to watch the coronation of Queen Elizabeth II of England. We didn't know at the time that the U.S. networks that covered the event didn't cover it directly. Instead, they pointed film cameras at BBC Television coverage and filmed the television coverage.

They weren't even using TV cameras. They were using film and had to develop the film before they could show it on TV. In the case of the coronation, they developed the film right away, bringing it to the United States in specially designed airplanes so it could be put on the air immediately.

That's a lot like some of the technology of the Web right now. We're cobbling together different technologies to try to make things work. We know it's going to be different later. We've already got our eye on the parallels with commercial television satellites and cable networks and so forth, but right now we're still piecing things together.

After we got our television, we used to invite people over to watch with us. We didn't even tell them what was on. And they didn't ask because it didn't matter: just watching TV was the attraction.

I carried this to rather ridiculous extremes. Early on Saturday mornings I'd go downstairs and watch test patterns. (Later, I felt foolish about this until I found out that most people my age have admitted to doing it too.)"

That happens now with lots of newcomers to the Net. They're not there for a specific purpose; they're just looking around. We call it "surfing." They surf indiscriminately just looking for interesting sites, newsgroups and so forth.

After a couple of months, they start looking for specific sites and particular sources of interest. That lasts for a couple of months as well. After that, people start using the Net and the Web for a specific purpose. They accomplish that purpose and then get back to other parts of their business.

But note that their business changes. Often when I'm asked how much time I spend online, I ask in return, "How much time do you spend on the telephone?" The issue isn't how much time you spend on the Net but rather whether it helps you accomplish your objectives more effectively and profitably.

Let's get back to our television analogy. In 1953 when television's growth started, it was in much the same shape as the Web is now. In other words, most of the innovations were still to be made, and most of the growth was still in the future.

Then came the battles over television technical standards. Companies knew that if they could get their standard accepted as "the" standard, they would make a lot of money. So they competed to try to set the technical standard.

In the early 1950s, for example, there were three different color television standards competing for prominence. Compare that to today's World Wide Web. The Web is the point-and-click, graphical access to the Internet. And to do it, you need a type of program called a browser.

Now, there are lots of ways that browsers can work and several different companies that make browsers. In 1996, we're seeing a lot of competition among these companies to be the standard browser.

There was also a lot of talk and debate about the role of government in regulating television. You'll hear similar discussion now regarding the Net and the Web as well as discussion about their ethical use. Most important to you if you're a business person is that we had to learn to use television for business, and we'll have to do the same with the World Wide Web. Go back and look at some old television advertising. Ads from the early 1950s weren't really television ads at all, at least not as we think of them now. The ads from that period pretty much fall into two groups. They're either print ads with added sound or radio ads with added pictures.

The same things are happening right now on the World Wide Web. We're still adapting models from other areas to fit the Web, and we haven't completed the integration. In the next 10 years, we'll start coming up with unique ways to enhance and do business on the Web that are not merely extensions and combinations of older models.

You can also expect a lot more technical innovation as we learn how to do things better and more effectively.

We've hit what the futurist Dan Burrus calls the flash point, that place where price and performance get to the level at which people get excited and start using the technology.

Let's swing for a minute to look at Web history and determine why that's happening right now and what it means to you as a business person.

What we now call the "Internet" was created during the Cold War. It was originally a way to link up research, academic and military sites to share information, and it did that pretty well.

In the beginning the Internet was funded by the government. By 1989, there were 600,000 people on this government-funded network. But there was no commercial activity until a company called Performance Systems International (PSI) established the first commercial links.

The Net at that time was described by several people as "the world's largest library with all the books thrown on the floor and the card catalog burned."

Beginning in 1991 things started to get easier. That was the year that folks at the University of Minnesota invented a tool called "Gopher." They named it after the mascot of the University of Minnesota, and it was a menu-based search tool. For the first time, people could begin to find information from the tremendous resources out there on the Net.

Why didn't people need this help before? Simple. Before this, the community of users was small enough and specialized enough that they could find what they wanted simply by asking other people that they knew. With commercial activity and with more people starting to investigate the Internet for other purposes, people could no longer find what they needed just by asking around.

One holdover from the old days is the basic structure of the Internet itself. The Internet has no center or multiple routing possibilities. It was built that way so its information would be protected in the case of a nuclear attack. With no center, there was no one place from which someone could eliminate the entire communications system. And with no multiple routing possibilities, huge chunks of the communication system could be lost, and the system could still function. Both characteristics are true of the Internet today.

And no one is "in charge" of the Internet. That's been both good and bad for business. With no one in charge, there is no one place from which to make decisions to "make the trains run on time." On the other hand, the fact that there's no central activity but lots of routes for getting things done has fostered a tremendous amount of innovation and creative thought that helps make the system function better.

But let's go back to 1991. That was when the first really effective search tools were invented. In 1992 a software engineer working at a particle physics laboratory in Switzerland needed to share information with people and keep track of the progress of his own projects.

The engineer was Tim Berners-Lee, and what he came up is something called "Hyperlinks." You know Hyperlinks if you have a Mac or Windows system and you've ever used a help file. On those help menus certain words look different from other words. Usually they're in a different color with an underline. If you click your mouse on one of those words, you'll jump to another part of the file, perhaps a definition.

What you experience at that point is "Hyperlinking." In this case, we call the result "Hypertext" because the software is linking between two pieces of text. But Hyperlink can link between text and programs, computers and functions and all manner of things. And it's not limited to linking in just one file. The technology can link functions and items in computers around the world using the Internet as the medium for the link.

Hyperlinking is the basic technology that makes the World Wide Web possible.

Hyperlinking has two powerful characteristics that may be important to you. First, it's what software folks call "not platform dependent." That means that you don't have to have a particular kind of computer to use Hyperlink technology. You can get to the World Wide Web whether you're using your company mainframe system, a PC, a Mac or just about anything else that can handle the basic communications functions.

The second powerful characteristic of Hyperlinking is that it works much the same way people think. When we consider a concept or try to solve a problem, our minds leap from one thing to another. One prominent brain researcher, in fact, has called the human brain "nature's connection-making engine." Hyperlinking works the same way.

Okay, that was 1992. Hyperlinking was neat but it was still text-based. In other words, you had to know the commands to get the thing to work. In 1993 a student at the University of Illinois, Marc Andreesen, invented a program called "Mosaic." Mosaic is a program you need to access Hyperlinks; it's called a "browser."

But it's a special kind of browser: it's a graphical browser. The best analogy for the difference between a regular browser and a graphical browser is the difference between DOS and Windows.

DOS is a text-based system. To give commands in DOS you must type in the commands. Windows replaces the need for typing in those commands with the ability to see pictures and use a mouse to click on pictures to get things done.

That's what Mosaic did for the Net. All of a sudden, using the Internet was easy enough that most people of moderate computer literacy and normal intelligence could get to the resources it had out there. But Mosaic still wasn't enough.

Mosaic was made available as freeware: you didn't have to pay for it. But you did have to be able to find it on the Net and download it to your computer or find a friend who had it and get that friend to install it for you. The documentation was written by and for programmers; since normal business people weren't familiar with the jargon, they had trouble wading through it.

In 1994 even jargon barriers disintegrated. In October of 1994, Spry (now a division of CompuServe) introduced a product called "Internet in a Box." That product was the first commercial graphical browser. It allowed business people like you and me to go to the store and buy software to find what we needed on the Net. The software was even complete with documentation and a help line. It got us started.

While all this was going on, commercial online services like America Online had been making things easier to use. They provided software to go online with their services free of charge. And the software, especially in America Online's case, was very user-friendly. For the first time it was possible for someone who was familiar with a computer but not with the online world to take a piece of software, install it in their computer and make the initial connection to an online service without any fat manuals or special help. Even more, once they got online, it was easy to find information and complete the tasks they wanted to complete.

Wow. What's happened now is that things have moved very fast, and more people—people you want to reach—have started showing up online.

Here's a brief comparison. In mid-1994, demographic surveys showed that Internet users were on average under 30, they had a household income under $30,000, and 90 percent were male. By the end of 1995, just 18 months later, the average age increased into the 30s; household income increased (according to some surveys) into the $50,000+ range; and the male/female percentage was 67 percent male, 33 percent female.

What's starting to change at this, the beginning of the rapid growth phase of the Internet and the World Wide Web, is the very makeup of the Net. Increasingly, the community online is representative of the upscale community in the population as a whole. Online users are more likely to be educated economically upscale than people not online. In fact, in one study of affluent Americans, 39 percent of households with more than $100,000 in household income had members on the Internet.

What can you expect in the future? You can expect more people to have computers. Already a vast majority of businesses use computers.

About a third of U.S. households have computers, and that will increase dramatically.

You can expect that more of the computers will be Net- and multimedia-capable. In the last couple of years, retailers have commonly bundled CD ROM, multimedia capability, modems and software together with computer systems. Businesses that already have local area networks are increasingly adding outside communication capability.

Because of the two things we've just mentioned, more and more of the people you want to do business with will be showing up on the Net and the Web. And businesses, perhaps including yours, will be there to meet and woo them.

Just as with the beginning of the adoption of television, we're in for an exciting time. In this case we're in for a lot of excitement because we're starting to use a technology that allows people operate the way they think on a truly global basis. The human mind works by making connections between bits of information. In your head, you jump from one thought or idea to another with the greatest of ease. The World Wide Web, technologically, does the same thing.

As late as the end of 1994, we were telling our clients and our audiences that the wave was coming, but they didn't have to act yet. Now it's different. They need to act.

This wave of adoption and this change of business will happen—with you or without you. Your options are to participate or not. Fortunately, it's getting easy to participate.

In this book we'll lay out what we know right now and what we can reasonably expect in the next few years about doing business online. We're far enough into the adoption phase that we can actually show you six specific models for doing business online that you can mix and match to serve your own strategic purpose.

We'll also discuss the basic tools and technologies available as well as the core strategies (the five *I*s of doing business online) you'll want to know to be effective.

Then we'll move into chapters dealing with specific business functions, like sales, marketing, distribution, customer service, production and product development. From these chapters you can learn the best ways to perform or enhance such functions online. We'll finish with a look at what you can expect in years ahead.

Before we go on, though, take a minute to think about why you're reading this book in the first place. What's your business purpose? What is it that you do in business? If you have these answers clearly in mind, reading this book will be productive for you: you'll be able to take your knowledge of your business and add the tools and techniques we talk about to explore many creative possibilities.

Okay, then, let's get started. With your business purpose firmly in mind, let's look at how the Internet and the World Wide Web can help serve that purpose and improve your business.

Chapter 2

Basic Technologies

Key points

- There are three technologies you should know about to do business online: the equipment you need to get connected, the place online where you'll do business (work sites) and the tools you'll use when you visit those places.

- Everything you do should support your strategic business purpose.

- You'll need equipment with multimedia capability to handle large sound and visual files.

- You'll need a good connection, a high-speed modem to connect yourself and more sophisticated tools to connect your business.

- You need browser software to connect to the Web. You'll also need software for electronic mail and other functions. There are many options for these.

- Commercial gateways are proprietary services connected to the Internet. They include America Online, CompuServe and Microsoft Network among others.

- Commercial gateways are services many folks use to make their first connection to the online world.

- Electronic mail (e-mail) is one of the simplest tools to use and yet one of the most powerful.

- Commercial gateways offer a variety of business possibilities especially for gathering information and connecting with other people.

- If a commercial gateway has a particular group of people or information source valuable to you, having an account there will probably be worthwhile.

- Most businesses connect to the Internet and Web through an Internet service-provider, which is faster, easier and less expensive than going through a commercial gateway.

- When you choose an Internet service-provider you should ask questions about connectivity and capability; also pay attention to its compatibility with you and your business.

- Direct connections to the Internet require major attention to security and often entail significantly higher telephone costs than going through an Internet Service-provider.

- You can set up your company presence on the World Wide Web several different ways depending on where you store pages and whether you use internal or outside help for either design or maintenance.

- Many companies are setting up internal Web sites using the same technology as the World Wide Web to share company information among members of the organization.

- An auto responder is a system that sends a designated file via e-mail in response to a properly formatted e-mail request.

- As an individual, you'll use autoresponders to get files of interest to you that others make available in this way. From a business standpoint, autoresponders are an excellent way to send information to people who want it.

- Mailing lists, also called listservs, are systems in which a message sent by one participant on a list automatically goes to the other participants on that list. They're used for discussing issues and getting out information.

- A database is an ordered and searchable collection of information. Most businesspeople use online databases to find articles in journals that relate to a topic of interest.

- - - - - - - -

- Forums and newsgroups are digital ways for people to discuss a common interest. The difference between the two depends on where you find them. A forum is on a commercial gateway like CompuServe, America Online or Prodigy. A newsgroup is on a portion of the Internet called "USENET."

- The Internet gives a powerful tool for keeping up with events and issues in your field: the electronic clipping service.

- Master Web search tools to get the most out of the Web.

- In the rest of this book, you'll work at developing your understanding of the various work sites and your skill with various online tools to do your business functions more effectively.

Management guru Peter Drucker defines *technology* as "the application of knowledge to useful work." A technology is a set of tools you use to accomplish the strategic ends you desire for your business.

In this chapter we'll talk about three topics related to basic technologies. We'll begin by discussing the equipment you need to be connected. That equipment may already be sitting in your office, or this chapter may serve as a purchasing guide.

Next, we'll look at different places online where you'll do business. You can think of them as "work sites." They include the commercial online services such as CompuServe and America Online, the Internet, the World Wide Web or internal Web sites.

Finally, we'll discuss the tools you'll use when you visit those work sites. You need these things in your toolbox to be effective. They include basic tools like electronic mail and an array of other tools you'll need to master to be successful online.

Equipment

This is not a computer book. It's a book about business. Nevertheless, we need to take a moment to lay out the basic equipment you'll need for varying levels of activity on the information superhighway. Regardless of where you're jumping onto the information superhighway, you'll need a computer. Just about any recently purchased computer will do. In fact, the power of the information highway comes from not being tied to one particular computer platform. Therefore, it doesn't matter if you've got a PC or a Mac or if your computer has a sophisticated network tied into a UNIX system. You need a computer to manipulate the information and to run the software you'll need when you get online.

A couple of other things will make your online experience more enjoyable and profitable, though. As we've said, more and more business activity conducted on the information highway is happening on the World Wide Web. One of the strengths of the Web is that it is a multimedia environment. In other words, more than just computer programs are out there, you can also find pictures and sound.

Well, if you know much about computer files, you know that picture-and-sound files are much bigger than standard, old text-and-information files. Those big files need to be manipulated, and the best way to do that is to make sure your computer system has as much random access memory (RAM) as possible. As one computer consultant friend of ours once said, "You can't be too rich, too thin or have too much RAM."

In the same vein, you'll probably want a multimedia-equipped computer. If you've bought a computer in the last couple of years, it's likely multimedia-equipped. Most of the systems sold to individuals nowadays have CD ROMs that can handle video and sound. That will be more-than-sufficient for the stuff you'll find out there on the Web.

Business computers may not be multimedia-capable. Recent studies have indicated that business is adopting multimedia-capable, or CD ROM-equipped, computers at a far slower rate than households.

If you're going to go on the Web, where sound and pictures are important, then your computer should have multimedia capability.

How large a hard drive do you need? There are a couple of ways to answer that one. The first is that nobody ever seems to have a large enough hard drive. So get the biggest one you can and figure that you'll still run out of space soon.

The other answer, though, is that many of the things you'll be doing on the Web won't require you to load up your hard drive with lots of files. You'll be able to find the information when you want it without keeping it on your computer all the time.

Storing Web information is a lot like the way we used to store food. For centuries, if you wanted to eat, you had store all you food right there at home. If it wasn't there, you didn't eat.

In the 20th century, we've developed food distribution to high art. On your way home from work, you can stop by your local supermarket and pick up the makings of a gourmet dinner. Since food is so readily available, you don't have to store the makings for that dinner around the house. And you don't need all that storage space.

The same is true for lots of information on the Web. If it's out there on the Web and you can get to it easily, you don't have to store all that information on your hard drive.

So which is the better answer about hard drive space? We really don't know. But we know that it's not a significant question. If you've got a multimedia-capable computer with enough random access memory to handle the multimedia tasks and it's multimedia-capable in other ways, Then things should be just fine.

You'll also need a modem. A modem is a piece of equipment that translates the digital language that your computer speaks into the analog language your telephone line needs to transmit. At the other end of the wire, another modem retranslates the analog telephone signal into a digital signal another computer can deal with.

If your company has a local area network, you'll need to address the issue of how you'll connect the modems to the phone line and whether they'll be available to the entire network or only to select stations.

Modems are rated in terms of speed, and as with other things in the computer world, bigger numbers here are better numbers. You'll hear the speed referred to as either "baud" rate or "BPS," which stands for "bits per second." There's a technical difference between the two, but you don't really need to know it since the people who'll sell you modems may not even know it. So a modem is referred to as 14,400 baud or a 14,400 BPS modem.

You should know a couple of things about modems if you are setting up a system to access the Net and the Web. A modem that is slower will not transfer information from the Net to your computer as rapidly as a faster modem. The result of that, in practical terms, is that for most people, the experience is too slow to be worth their time. That makes 14,400 the minimum speed you should have to handle access to the Internet and World Wide Web.

Several important developments will occur in this area in the next year or so, but a good modem at 28,800 will probably be sufficient.

You'll also need software, specifically, a program called a "browser," to use the World Wide Web. Netscape is the most popular browser on the Web right now. Other browsers are variants of the original Mosaic program.

You'll also need a program that handles electronic mail. Make sure you get one that will let you read your mail and prepare answers while you're not online. You'll find that you give better replies that way, and you'll save money in online connection costs.

You'll probably also want two other types of programs. You should have what's called a "terminal" program to handle some tasks you'll find on the Net that a browser or your e-mail program can't handle. A terminal program allows your computer to act like a terminal for a remote computer that you are connecting to over the Net. For example, a terminal program will allow you to use your modem and a phone line to dial up many university libraries and check their card catalogs. That same terminal program will let you do the same thing over the Internet for the university library systems as vast as that of the University of California.

Frankly, most business users don't use these programs very much, but you need to know that they exist, and you need to have them available if you do need them.

If you're already on a network, your systems administrator can help you pick the right software. If you're signing up with an Internet service-provider, often software is provided as a part of the package.

Up until very recently, you had to put together a collection of these programs yourself since they didn't come bundled very effectively. Now we're seeing the introduction of Internet suites. A "suite" in the software world is a collection of programs designed to work together. The first of these was the Quarterdeck Internet Suite, but look for other manufacturers to put together packages of programs that handle Web and Net access and work cleanly and easily together.

Be sure that you look for programs that work well for you. There are two things to consider. First, find programs that perform all the functions that you want to perform. If you need an e-mail program that allows you to sort messages in different ways, you need to make sure that function is in the e-mail program you purchase. In addition, you also want to make sure that you're comfortable with a program. There are different programs that may have a function you want but you need to find one that is easy for you to use. That's a matter of personal preference, not technological specification.

Those are pretty much the basics in terms of a computer, modem and software. If you're connecting to the Web yourself, you'll need to pick these things and take care of the details yourself. If you've got a systems administrator or an IS department at work, look for some help there. But don't let the technical types overwhelm you with their jargon. In this book and others, you'll find out what you can do online. Once you decide what you want to do, tell those technical types what you want and ask them how to do it.

When you've got the gear together, you'll next need to address how you're going to connect to the information superhighway.

Work sites

There are lots of different work sites out there along the information highway. These are the places that you go to do your business.

Commercial gateways (CompuServe, America Online, Prodigy or others) are part of the Internet but offer special services and benefits to their own subscribers not available to others. Think of commercial gateways as separate networks connected to a network of networks: the Internet.

Another work site is the World Wide Web. This is the point-and-click multimedia part of the Internet. Increasingly, the World Wide Web is also where many Internet functions come together. For example, Web sites increasingly have ways for you to send e-mail to the owner of the site. They have ways for you to request files via File Transfer Protocol with the click of a button.

A final type of work site is an internal Web site. Many companies are now taking the Hyperlink technology developed originally for the World Wide Web and setting up internal Web sites. These are not part of the Internet at all but are part of an internal computer network. Internal Web sites are great ways to share company information in a multimedia format and link information in ways that people can use it effectively.

On the IBM Corporation's internal Web site (Intranet), for example, there are pages devoted to different company locations. An employee who is traveling to a place he or she has not visited before can see pictures of the buildings, maps of the location and get directions from the airport from the internal Web site. He or she can also, in many cases, find a Web page on the person who is going to be visited, and read the biography and find a picture. The Hyperlink technology makes these functions far easier than they would be if the visitor had to obtain different paper files from a variety of locations and read each one separately.

Because commercial gateways are most likely the way you'll begin to access the Net, let's discuss these work sites further. The commercial gateways are CompuServe, America Online, Prodigy, the Microsoft Network, eWorld, Delphi or others. With a subscription to any of these, you'll get an electronic mail address and the ability to send e-mail across the Internet.

In addition, you'll get certain special services only subscribers get.

Each of the commercial gateways offers forums: places online where people with a common interest discuss that interest. They also offer ways for subscribers to buy things, information sources, publications such as newspapers and magazines and, of course, a gateway to the World Wide Web and Internet.

America Online is the largest of the commercial gateways, and for the last few years, it's also been the fastest-growing. America Online's major strength is its ease of use and ability to set up real-time meetings online. America Online provides its own proprietary software and a network of phone connections around the country allowing you to connect to the Internet with a local phone call.

CompuServe is one of the oldest of the commercial gateways and also one of the largest. It offers excellent specialty forums in a variety of business, professional and personal interest areas. Because these forums have been active for so long, they tend to have excellent resource libraries connected with them. CompuServe also offers the best databases. CompuServe offers its own browser software, but you can get to CompuServe using any general communications software. CompuServe also offers special "auto pilot" packages to help you automate your forum and e-mail activity.

Delphi was once a major competitor of CompuServe and America Online. It was also the first commercial gateway to make a full connection to the Internet, but it never developed a graphical interface. Delphi gradually slipped further and further behind CIS and AOL.

- - - - - - - -

Delphi was then purchased by Rupert Murdock and merged into MCI's Internet strategy. Delphi will be attempting to make a comeback in the next couple of years. For now, it's a relatively small gateway with limited services.

And Genie is a gateway set up by General Electric. It's fairly small, in fact much smaller than any of the other services. For that reason, it doesn't have either the number of individuals or the number of information sources that are on the larger commercial gateways. The result of that is that unless it has a specific forum or information source that is valuable to you, Genie is not likely to be a good service for you to subscribe to.

The Microsoft Network is an emerging gateway that Microsoft has bundled with its Windows 95 program. In its early months, Microsoft Network went through several growing pains, but as these work out, we guess that Microsoft Network will be a major player in the online world.

When you're selecting a commercial gateway, look at whether it has specific services or forums that are important to you. If your business sells products to photographers, for example, you'll be interested in any online service that has a forum where photographers congregate online to discuss photography issues.

All commercial gateways run online marketing systems often called "electronic malls." If marketing your products and services turns out to be part of your strategy, then you'll want to evaluate this aspect of their services to determine what kind of business you can with each gateway.

You may want to use commercial gateways for personal and professional growth as well as for business. Even if only one offers what is best for your business, you may find that a mix of gateways serves all your needs best. You might find, for example, that you like reading *The New York Times* on AOL, that you get great information from professional forums on CompuServe and that there is a forum on another online service that's the only one that deals with your particular hobby. You might want a subscription to all three services.

Many of our clients and friends have a direct connection to the Internet and the World Wide Web but still maintain accounts on one or more of the commercial gateways. Many folks maintain CompuServe accounts for the quality of information in the forums and databases there. They may also maintain America Online accounts for the easy use of e-mail and other functions AOL offers.

A key rule here is that any gateway with a particular group of people or information source or publication that's valuable to you may be worth the subscription price for that resource alone.

The commercial gateways are also an easy and safe place to start exploring the Internet and the World Wide Web. If you're new to the online world, consider a subscription to a commercial gateway (America Online is probably the easiest to use) and begin your explorations of the Net and the Web from there.

Then, when you're ready, you'll be ready to set up your own account with an Internet service-provider.

People and businesses use Internet service-providers rather than the commercial gateways for lots of their Internet activity because the cost is lower and the performance is higher. When you're choosing an Internet service-provider, you need to feel comfortable with the provider, their expertise and how they relate to you. When choosing a provider for business purposes, you also need to ask the following questions.

Connectivity questions

- Can I get a good-quality, local telephone connection?
- Can I check my e-mail while I'm on the road without paying an exorbitant premium?

The answers to both of these questions should be yes before you select a provider. And don't ask just the service-providers. Talk to people using their services. Find out what experience others have had with the provider to see if the connections are regularly available and work well. And make sure you'll be able to connect both from home and from the road. Ask these questions even when a service-provider signs you up automatically for purchasing an Internet software package.

Ask what kind of phone line connection your provider has to the Internet. Listen for terms like "T1" and "T3." A T1 is a big information pipe. A T3 is a lot bigger than a T1. A serious Internet service-provider today will probably have a T3 line.

Ask about plans for upgrading the connection to deal with growth in the number of connections and with technological advances.

Integrated Services Digital Network (ISDN) connections will also be available in many areas. ISDN connections are somewhat attractive to businesses because they allow for faster data transfer. But there's a problem: The main problem most businesses have with ISDN connections is coordinating the installation and operation of equipment and software. If you're considering an ISDN connection, make sure you identify local folks who know the ropes to get you started.

If you're considering a direct connection to the Internet without using either a commercial gateway or a service-provider, you'll need to address security concerns such as constructing fire walls and limiting access using established rules. You'll need help with these. If you're a small business, check out the costs involved in the phone and security equipment, tasks and support people you'll need. Most smaller businesses (and many large businesses) find it more efficient and economical to stay with an Internet service-provider rather than set up direct connections.

Once you've addressed the connection issues, you'll want to ask another series of questions related to available business services.

Capability questions

We've established that if you're a small business, you'll probably be considering an Internet service-provider. Make sure it offers all the services you want, both now and in the future.

Make sure your provider offers:

• Domain name service.

• Autoresponder capability.

• Listserv capability to set up a mailing list.

We'll cover domain name service right here. We'll cover autoresponders and mailing lists in more detail later.

Large companies typically have direct connections to the Internet. They also have a domain name. A "domain name" is the language-like address that people use when they send e-mail to people at a particular company.

If your company has a computer that is also an Internet host, then you have a domain name. If you're a smaller organization connecting to the Net through a Internet service-provider, then you'll want a domain name to serve to establish your presence on the Internet. Why? With a domain name, people know you are serious. You'll put yourself on a more level playing field with larger companies.

Take this example. One of the largest publishers of computer books has the domain name "cmp.com." One of the authors of this book has the domain name "cyberpower.com." If you look at those two names side by side, you can't really tell which is the large company and which is the smaller. If you're looking to compete with larger organizations, a domain name can help level the playing field.

There are two ways to create an effective domain name: build it around your company name or build it around what you do.

You'll pay a fee for registering a domain name. For companies with direct connection or a systems administrator, generally the administrator will handle the registration process. If you're a smaller company going through an Internet service-provider, generally your service-provider will handle the registration. It will probably also mark up the basic fee to cover administrative costs. Though you might save some money handling registration yourself, most smaller- and medium-size businesses let their provider handle the registration because of the many technical details involved.

In addition to a registration fee, you'll pay an annual fee to maintain a domain name. Again, usually your provider will handle this.

By the way, the letters that appear at the end of a domain name are actually a carryover from the time when certain parts of the Net could not carry commercial activity. The letters helped identify which organizations were conducting commercial activity and which were associated with education or government.

The following are common extensions and their original meaning:

.com   commercial

.gov   government

.edu   education

.org   organization (often non-profit)

.mil   military

.net   net

These extensions are coming into wider use even though their original utility is diminished. In fact, they're becoming common even in countries with different organizational classifications or primary languages.

Your Internet service-provider should offer your business all the key services as well as new possibilities that may appear in the future. That's where compatibility comes in.

Compatibility

You should be comfortable with your Internet service-provider. After all, you're turning your business over to it. The best test for that is a gut test.

How do you feel when you deal with the folks there? Are you getting answers to your questions? Do they have good plans for keeping up with the growth of the Net and new services? If you can't answer these questions positively, then you should probably seek another provider.

World Wide Web

As we've described elsewhere, the World Wide Web consists of pictures that ride on the Internet and help you use a point-and-click program called a browser to get at information and contacts that you want.

You can connect to the Web in several ways. One way is to use the browser that comes with a commercial gateway such as America Online, CompuServe or Prodigy. Another is to use one of the larger national providers such as Pipeline or Netcom, which give you an integrated package including your electronic mail and a Web browser.

The problem with either of these alternatives, though, is that you must use the software provided by the service. You, however, might prefer a different browser. Another problem is that services such as AOL, CompuServe, Prodigy, Pipeline and Netcom have a limited number of newsgroups. They might not have a newsgroup that you want to participate in.

For those reasons, you and your company may want to look for an Internet Service Provider (ISP) to handle your connection to the

Internet. When you do that, you'll be able to pick a browser and e-mail program from among the many available that meets your needs and personal preferences.

You can always connect your company directly to the Internet without going through an ISP, but that has some problems. Direct connections result in dramatically higher telephone line costs and greater security concerns. In both cases, you'll need specialists either on staff or as outside consultants to help you figure out the best way to handle your connection.

If your company is big enough to consider a direct connection, you should have a systems administrator who can help you find the proper people, help and information. A good deal of this is actually available on the Web.

If you want to establish a Web presence by putting up a page or a Web site, you have the option of doing it yourself, with help or going to an Internet mall where lots of companies are grouped together.

You can maintain your own pages on the Web if you have direct access to the Web, perhaps through your Internet provider's computer or through a computer run by a company that specializes in Web services. For a more thorough discussion of issues related to putting up a Web page, see Appendix 2 on page 181.

Internal Web sites

We can't leave this work sites discussion without mentioning internal Web sites. Development of internal Web sites is a rapidly emerging usage of the Hyperlink technology that's got some real potential. A company sets up a Web site, but instead of putting it out on the World Wide Web for public consumption, it sets the site up on its own internal network. The technology involved with an internal Web site is the same as with the World Wide Web. The browsers you use for going out to the World Wide Web work just as effectively accessing files on your own computer.

In larger companies, internal Web sites have been used to maintain information about remote locations, to post a version of the company newsletter, to allow employees to put up individual pages so others can read about their backgrounds when they want or need to and to post information "online" about personnel issues, such as benefits, holidays, etc.

Many companies also consider an internal Web site an alternative to some of the more powerful, but more complex groupware programs such as Lotus Notes. In fact, the administrator at one large company described an internal Web as "Lotus Notes Lite." With an internal Web, people in your company hook up to your network and view specific information related to the company, its objectives, their co-workers, ideas or almost anything else that might be helpful. With an internal Web, that information is available whenever they have access to the network—pretty much anytime they're hooked up. Coupled with e-mail and mailing lists, which we'll discuss in a little bit, an internal Web site can be a great way to make sure information is distributed regardless of how geographically widespread a company's locations or how varied employees' schedules.

Tools

Once you get to a work site, a commercial gateway, the Internet, the World Wide Web or an internal Web site or network, you'll need certain tools. In the next few pages, we'll cover some of the most important tools, along with some of the things you really need to know to use them effectively. We'll discuss electronic mail, autoresponders, mailing lists, forums and newsgroups, databases, clipping services and World Wide Web search tools.

Electronic mail

Let's begin with e-mail. Electronic mail is one of the simplest tools to use, yet one of the most powerful. Basic use of e-mail is almost intuitive. When most people hook up to a network, whether its an internal or a world-spanning network, they pick up the basics of e-mail quickly and easily. Note we didn't say that they pick up all the tools for handling e-mail in the most effective way. That takes a bit more work.

If you're going to use e-mail effectively, you need to start by understanding that electronic mail is far more conversational than formal, written communication. This means that e-mail will tend to be less formal. But conversations with business colleagues are likely to be more formal than those with a friend.

There's one more small concern related to this formality issue. If you're doing business with people in different cultures, you need to adapt to the level of formality they are most accustomed to. American business communication, written or digital, is generally less formal than comparable communications in many other countries around the world. In addition to adjusting for whether it is business or personal and whether your communication is digital or letter, you also need to adjust for the culture of the person with whom you're communicating.

Let's look at some basic rules for effective e-mail communication.

Effective e-mail communication follows most of the same basic rules that effective written communication follows. Short words, short sentences, short paragraphs, headers that summarize, etc. All these make your writing easier to understand online just as they do in the world of letters and memos. A couple of things, though, are different online.

First, people view your message on a short computer screen. Computer screens are significantly shorter than sheets of paper. So the most important stuff must be where they'll see it first. That's the header and the first paragraph or two of your message. Figure on about 20 lines of message.

Second, electronic mail uses message headers or subject lines, and on most systems, people can scan those headers or subject lines to determine which messages they'll read and which ones they'll read first. If your message header doesn't tell people what your message is about, they' have no way of judging the importance or utility of your message. So make your headers descriptive.

In electronic mail, as with other written forms of communication, you have only words to convey a message. Studies by Dr. Albert Mehrabian and others indicate that about 93 percent of communication in a face-to-face situation comes from factors other than the words used. Meaning comes from gestures, tone of voice, facial expression, dress, demeanor and other verbal and nonverbal cues.

In electronic mail, none of those cues are available. However, experienced electronic mail users have developed a system of abbreviations and tiny symbols called "emoticons." "Emoticons" are often called "smileys" after the symbol that looks like this :-) and indicates a (sideways) smile. Use them to get the emotional component into your e-mail and other online communications. Here are a few of the more popular emoticons.

Emoticons

:-)   smile
:-(frown

Some people create them without the "nose" like :) and :(

;-)   winking
:-D   laughing
:-\   perplexed or skeptical

Some emoticons are just for fun.

8-)   smiley wearing glasses
*<|:-)   Santa Claus
@-->-->-   rose

Different newsgroups, forums and e-mail groups develop their own common smileys.

Abbreviations

As in the world of letters and memos, people develop abbreviations to say things in a shorter space. Here are common online abbreviations you'll see in newsgroups, forums or e-mail communications.

BTW   by the way

LOL   laughing out loud

ROFL   rolling on the floor laughing

PMFJI   pardon me for jumping in

TIA	thanks in advance
YMMV	your mileage may vary (different folks get different results)
IMHO	in my humble opinion (you can delete the H if it's not humble)
OTOH	on the other hand

And here's our personal favorite:

TLA	Three Letter Acronym

When you use electronic mail and reply to another person's message, common etiquette is to refer to that message briefly in one of the following two ways.

```
>This is the text of the message that you're
>making reference to.
```

or

```
>> This is the text of the message that you're
making reference to. <<
```

Some electronic mail software packages can automate parts of this for you.

If you're using electronic mail for business, especially if you're sending messages out across the Internet, you should also have something called a "sig" (for "signature") file. You'll need one of these because you have no letterhead in digital communication. A signature file functions as a combination letterhead and floating bulletin board, as you will see momentarily.

Many electronic mail systems will automate the process of including a signature file in your e-mail communication. If yours does not, you can set up a simple text file on your Windows or Mac machine that includes your signature file. Then, when you're in the process of creating e-mail, just cut and paste your signature to the message.

Here's the sig file used by one of the authors.

```
Wally Bock
Cyberpower Alert! electronic newsletter
http://www.bockinfo.com wbock@bockinfo.com
510-835-8566
```

Note that the sig is less than five lines long. It includes material about what Wally does, as well as contact information. That's the same kind of information that might be on your letterhead or business card.

A final word about e-mail. E-mail is an exceptionally powerful tool because it's quick and easy to use. Try to find ways to integrate electronic mail into all of your business communications processes.

For example, you can send an electronic thank-you note after a sales call in addition to a handwritten note. You can use the forwarding feature of most e-mail packages to send an article of interest to a client, prospect or colleague. You can use the list feature of many e-mail programs to get out a quick note to several people about an important item.

Autoresponders

An "autoresponder" is a system that sends a designated file by e-mail in response to an e-mail request. You'll also hear these referred to as "eback" systems or "mailbots."

You'll use autoresponders in business in two ways. As an individual, you'll use autoresponders to get files of interest to you that others make available in this way. Many people do this though their Web site. On a Web site such as this, you'll click on a button that says "Send File," and an auto responder system will send the file to you.

For your business, autoresponders are an excellent way to send information to people who want it. Do this in conjunction with your Web site and in other ways. With an autoresponder, people can get information about you and your business 24 hours a day and seven days a week. They can also get it whether or not they have access to the Web. To get information using an auto responder, all your prospects or customers need is electronic mail and the name or address of the file to request.

There are several different kinds of autoresponders, and your systems administrator or Internet service-provider can help you select which ones might be best.

Mailing lists

Mailing lists, also called "listservs," are systems in which a message sent by one participant on the list automatically goes to the other participants on the list. They're used for discussions of issues and for distributing information.

The name "listserv" comes from one of the three names of software that does this mailing list function. The others are called "listproc" and "majordomo."

Most of the mailing lists you'll encounter work like this. You "subscribe" by sending an electronic mail message to the owner of the list. Usually, but not always, you'll include in the message body the word "subscribe" and the name of the list.

For most mailing list subscriptions, you'll write something like this in the message body:

```
SUBSCRIBE LISTNAME
```

You will receive a message that tells you that you have been added to the list. With most lists, you'll also receive two other bits of information. One bit is called a "frequently asked question," or "FAQ," file. It will tell you the purpose of the list and the basic rules under which it operates.

The message you get when you subscribe also usually tells you how to remove your name from the list. For that reason, you'll want to keep this file. When and if you want your name removed, you'll need to know how since most of the processes are automated.

Once you're on a mailing list, you'll receive messages in your e-mail box from other participants in the list. They will send a message to the list (not the list owner), and everyone who subscribes to the list will get their message.

When you reply to a message, your reply goes to everyone on the list unless you make a special effort to send it as a private electronic mail message. Replies using the reply button will send your message to the entire list.

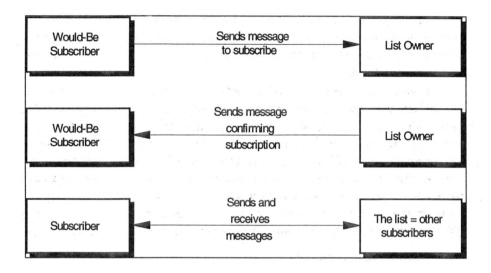

That's important enough to dwell on for a second. Many people new to mailing lists presume that their response to a mailing list message is a private e-mail message to the person who sent the note. Not so. Their response will be seen by everyone on the list. Lesson: Be very, very sure that what you want to say is suitable for public consumption. Think about how you'd feel if your message were plastered all over the newspapers in your town the next day. In fact, with larger lists more people will see it on the Internet than they ever would in your newspaper.

We've just outlined the basic ways mailing lists work. Some mailing lists put a couple of simple variations on this. Some mailing lists do not use the automated sign-up features available. They screen mailing list participants or check credentials. Several professional lists such as SPJ-L, the list for the Society of Professional Journalists, are like this.

Some lists are also moderated lists. That means postings are reviewed by a moderator before they are sent to the entire list. Again, these tend to be lists for various professional areas.

Finally, some companies use mailing lists as a one-way distribution tool: they send out information but don't allow others on the list to reply to the list as a whole.

You may use mailing lists a couple of ways. As an individual, you'll use a mailing list as a participant in discussions of generally business, professional or personal interests. Mailing lists exist for just about every interest.

The best way to find mailing lists or newsgroups is to get references from your friends who are already online. Start by asking the folks you know what newsgroups or mailing lists they subscribe to. Then try them yourself. You'll also find that your online friends will refer to newsgroups or mailing lists that they use. Try them out too. And browse the list of what's available on whatever service you use to get to the Internet. Try any newsgroup that looks interesting. Listings of newsgroups and mailing lists are readily available. One list of mailing lists has more than 5,000 and is available by sending e-mail to:

listserv@listserv.net

with `LIST GLOBAL` in the message body.

Five thousand is a lot of lists to go through, though, and we still like the "referral method" best.

For your business you can set up a mailing list. This is called "sponsoring" a mailing list, and it's a way to discuss issues that your clients, customers and friends would be interested in. Discussing issues can be a great public relations tool and a way to get lots of feedback. We'll hit those kinds of applications throughout this book.

You can also use the mailing list technology internally as a way for employees to keep up with each other and share ideas and successes.

When you participate in newsgroups and mailing lists, you'll use the e-mail tools we've just discussed. The same rules for messages, replies and the use of a .sig file are important. You'll also learn to weave subtle mentions of what you do into your messages as a way of raising list participants' awareness of what you do, so when they are interested in what you have to offer, they'll know to contact you.

Newsgroups and forums

In some ways newsgroups and forums are very much like mailing lists. They involve messages posted for a group of "subscribers" or "members" to read and reply to. They're generally organized around topics of interest: professional, business and recreational.

Both forums and newsgroups are digital ways for people with a common interest to discuss that interest. The difference between them is where you find them. A forum exists on a commercial gateway like CompuServe, America Online or Prodigy. A newsgroup is on a portion of the Internet called "USENET."

Actually, the term "newsgroup" is not correct. These are really discussion groups. Whereas mailing lists involve messages that come to you by electronic mail, forums and newsgroups put the messages in a "place" to which you go. For example, if you are participating in the forum on CompuServe called PRSIG, you go to PRSIG when you sign on to CompuServe to see what messages have been posted since your last visit.

Messages on forums and newsgroups are "threaded." This means that when you read the messages, you'll read them in chronological order starting with the original message (if you haven't already read it) followed by the replies in the order they were posted.

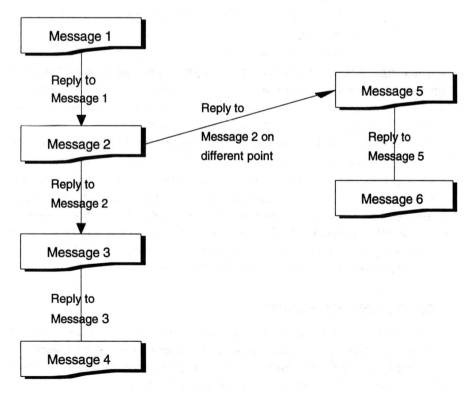

You'll use forums and newsgroups for business much like you use mailing lists: as a way of gathering ideas and information. Which is better, mailing lists or forums and newsgroups? The answer seems to depend on personal preference—if you have a choice. In some cases, only one forum, newsgroup or mailing list exists on a particular topic.

In many cases, though, you'll be able to pick from several different forums or newsgroups. If you prefer to participate via electronic mail and have it come to you, you'll probably like mailing lists more. On the other hand, if you prefer going to get your messages and the threaded presentation, you'll probably like forums and newsgroups.

Here's a tip: If you have the option of having several e-mail addresses, you might have your mailing list messages sent to a different e-mail address or to a different user name than your regular e-mail. Then messages from a mailing list won't clog up your e-mail box, and you'll be able to get them when you choose.

You may use forums and newsgroups for some of the self-promotion activities we'll suggest in this book, but unless you work for a fairly large company, you probably won't be sponsoring a forum or newsgroup. What's more, forums and newsgroups require an approval process and in the case of forums on the commercial gateways, a payment of fees. But setting up a mailing list just takes the right software.

Clipping services

One of the most powerful "keeping-up" tools the online world makes available to you is an array of different clipping services. In the off-line world years back, a clipping service consisted of a bunch of people sitting around in a room checking papers for mentions of a particular company or a particular topic. When they found a mention, they'd clip out the story and send it to whoever was paying for the subscription and looking for the information.

That's pretty much what digital clipping services do too. The difference is that computers are much better at the scanning and clipping than people are. Computers don't get bored. Computers will check everything. Computers have a broader reach. Computers read more quickly.

Most clipping services are organized around the news wires over which most news today flows. They've been called news wires since the days when the information actually flowed over telegraphic wires. Today, however, most stories are filed digitally and transmitted from a news service to a newspaper or from one paper to another over the Net. Clipping services give you the ability to scan the same news wires that newspapers scan. Here are some examples of different types of clipping services.

Heads Up is a service of Individual, Inc. For a monthly fee, you receive—daily by fax or in your e-mail box—a description of stories that match categories you've selected. Heads Up is a "fixed category" service. That means you pick from among predetermined categories.

Once you've scanned information on various stories, you can to request an entire story.

Another clipping service that's in fairly common use is the one connected with the executive option on CompuServe. This goes by the name of "Executive News Service." With it you can set up as many as four folders that will scan news wires from among the several you have as options for your particular key words.

To get the stories, you sign on to CompuServe and go to your clipping folders. Then you have the option to preview the stories and read them or download any that you find interesting.

A third news service is News Hound, a service of the *San Jose Mercury News*. News Hound charges you a monthly fee for which you can set up as many as five profiles. You choose the words a story may and must have as well as a degree of fit between the news stories and your ideal profile. Then the service scans a variety of news wires for you.

When it finds stories that match your profile, they are e-mailed to you usually within an hour of when they hit the wire.

Finally, there's Net News, a service offered by Stanford University. Net News is free. It is not a news-clipping service in the sense we've discussed so far. But it is one you'll be interested in knowing about. Net News scans USENET newsgroups looking for your key words and then sends you frequent lists of mentions matching your profile that have appeared across various newsgroups. You have the option to get the entire posting if you choose.

Clipping services are a way for you to keep up with critical information in your field or to track competition. They're one of the most powerful, helpful, inexpensive and easy things you can do online.

Databases

A database is an ordered and searchable collection of information. The card catalog in your public library is a database. The computer file listing your customers is a database. There are databases online that include information you'd like to have.

Most businesspeople use online databases to find articles in journals that relate to a topic of interest. That topic can be a subject, an issue or a company.

Databases online are available in basically two ways. First, they're available through specialized services such as Dialog and News Net. There are also services like Lexis/Nexis. What all these have in common is that they index an array of bibliographical sources and allow you to search for what interests you.

The search process is something like the searches you used to do in the library. The difference is that the computer searches more quickly and over a broader range than you can even imagine.

One of the authors of this book used to spend two days a month in a major business and social science library at the University of California at Berkeley to keep up on management and marketing issues relevant to his work. In that time, he would check the tables of contents of the two hundred or so journals to which this major library subscribed. Then he'd copy articles of interest and attempt to read the ones that were most important.

He still does that kind of searching but not in the library anymore. Today he uses the knowledge index feature on CompuServe to search a database called "ABI/INFORM." Instead of two hundred or so journals, he's now scanning over a thousand. ABI/INFORM also provides article abstracts, so he can easily tell which ones are most valuable. In fact, many times the abstract mentions the key fact or finding of an article, and the entire article is not needed.

Another benefit of online database searches is that the results are available in digital form. This means that quoting from an article is a matter of cutting and pasting rather than copying by hand or copy machine. And because the text is in digital form, it's also searchable with a variety of computer tools.

Oh yes, there is one more benefit. Instead of two days, the search now takes about 15 minutes.

Database searching is an art in itself, but you as a business person in the information age need to become comfortable with basic search techniques and tools. We'd recommend that you spend some of your online time learning about simple databases that you can search and getting the most from them.

Web search tools

Later in this book, we'll be talking more about Web sites. We've already discussed the first tool you'll need to search for information on the World Wide Web: a software program called a "browser." You'll probably have a graphical browser like Mosaic, Netscape, Net Cruiser or Quarterdeck Mosaic.

You should become familiar with your browser and how it works. You might also check into several books on the market that give browsing tips and lists of sites you can check. For right now, let's assume you will pick up the basics of using your browser and you're ready to find things on the Web. For this you'll need Web search tools.

You may hear these referred to as "search engines" or "search utilities." Whatever name you hear, they do a single, simple, thing. They give you a way to find what you're looking for on the Web. Using search tools is fairly simple. You put the word or words you're searching for in the space provided. You select any options a particular search tool gives you to choose from, and then you see what you get back.

You find things on the Web via their URL. This stands for Uniform Resource Locator and it's a lot like an address. (See page 179.) Six commonly used search tools (with their URL addresses) are:

Yahoo	http://www.yahoo.com
WebCrawler	http://www.webcrawler.com
Lycos	http://www.lycos.com
InfoSeek	http://www.infoseek.com
Magellan	http://www.mckinley.com
AltaVista	http://www.altavista.digital.com

From a business standpoint, you need to know two things. First, not all the search tools index the same things or in the same way. So if you're looking for information or a company name, you should look in several different places.

Second, if your company wants its Web pages to be listed with these search utilities, you will need to take the step of registering with the individual utilities. That entails having someone go to the search utility and fill out an available form for registration. There are also companies whose business is registering Web sites on a variety of search utilities. Your company may want to make a determination about whether you should use one of these registration service companies as a more cost-effective way to get the registration done.

In the last couple of years we've seen a move toward automatic indexing systems. These search engines use programs that are variously called "spiders" or "worms." These programs automatically search the Net for new Web pages. When they find them, they gather the information on the page and index the page. The information they gather is added to the search engine's index. You will see more of these in the future.

How do search engines make the money necessary to keep operating? Many of them support themselves primarily through advertising. Some charge modest fees for searches. You can expect that some will be charging fees for registration in the future and that there may be special fees for special classes of registration. That would mean, for example, that you would pay extra to always be in the first 25 sites related to particular search words. For that you'd pay an extra fee.

As a businessperson, though, you'll want to take control of some of the registration process. Ask your systems administrator or your Web site designers to make sure your company is utilizing all the tricks to get its Web pages registered in the best possible way.

Most of the indexing systems index either simply the title of a Web page or the items at the top of a Web page. Obviously, that means you'll want the important stuff in those spots so it will be indexed as specifically as possible.

There are more details and tips for registering Web pages in the appendix section on building a business Web site.

Conclusion

That's your array of work sites and tools. If you'll be doing business online, you need at least a working knowledge of what the different sites and tools are and how they're likely to help you meet your business goals. But don't get overwhelmed with the technology. You'll find that someone who can help you with the technical issues is always around. Your job as a business person is to learn how the tools and techniques and sites and ideas apply to your business purpose and fit into your overall business strategy.

There used to be a service in the Bay Area in California called "Rent-A-Geek" that provided knowledgeable "computer geeks" to help people set up systems and so forth.

You may not have such a service where you live and work, but you'll find no shortage of highly knowledgeable technical people. What you are likely to find is that those technical people understand the technology superbly but not its possible business applications.

As you move through the rest of this book, your challenge will be to connect what you know about business with what you're learning about the technologies, tools and places that you can operate online. You'll be the translator, the person standing between the purely-businesspeople on one side and the technological people on the other side. Think about this as we move to our next chapter, where we'll talk about basic techniques and strategies.

Chapter 3

Basic Techniques
and Strategies

Key points

- There are six basic models for doing business online.
- You can use the Internet and the World Wide Web to sell things to individuals or other businesses.
- You can offer subscriptions or memberships in which individuals or businesses pay a fee to receive special benefits or information to which only they have access.
- You can sell advertising on your Web site, if it is a popular one.
- You can provide direct Web services such as server space, page design, administrative help, consulting, etc.
- You can reduce costs by using Net and Web tools to automate many business functions.
- You can use Net and Web tools to enhance business operations that are not themselves on the Net.
- Your challenge as a business person is to pick the best combination of models for your strategic purpose.
- There are five basic strategies you'll use to achieve maximum business success.

- You can provide lots of relevant information to people you want to influence.
- You can give people new ways to interact with you.
- You can integrate your online business activities with your other business activities in support of your strategic goals.

In the opening chapter to this book, we discussed the fact that the adoption of the Internet and the World Wide Web for business is similar to businesses' adoption of television in the early 1950s. Businesses are far enough along in the adoption process now that we can begin to see the different ways people are using the Internet and the World Wide Web to do business. In this chapter we'll talk about six basic models for doing business online and the five basic strategy considerations, what we call the five I's, of doing business online.

Think about how what we discuss might relate to your business. Think about the basic models as things you can do and the strategies as ways to do them effectively.

Six online business models

Before we start, let's refresh your memory on a basic equation.

Revenue = Income - Expenses

We thought reminding you of that equation was important because most of the material written so far about doing business on the Internet and the Web has concentrated on the idea of selling and marketing. There's a lot more to doing business than just selling and marketing.

Sure, selling and marketing are important; they enhance the revenue side of the equation, and bringing up revenues is a way to bring up profits. But cutting down on expenses can improve your profitability as well, and there are ways to do that online.

Also, much of the material you may have read about doing business online seems to treat the online business as a separate business. It seems to say that what you do online is different and separate from what you do with the rest of your business. That's simply not true.

As you begin thinking about how to use the Net and the Web in your business, you'll need to figure out how they fit into the overall structure and purpose of your business. Anything you do with online business needs to serve your overall business purpose.

With our basic profit equation in mind, let's take a quick look at the six business models.

Direct sales is one model. People are now selling things on the Net and the Web. Take AllWeather, Inc., which has sold well over half a million dollars in orders for its swimming pool alarm.

Subscriptions is another model. In the subscription model, fees are charged to one group of people (often called "subscribers" or "members") for services, information or products they have access to but others do not. Publications like the *San Jose Mercury News* have led the way, and businesses like InfoSeek and many associations use the model to generate revenue.

A third model for doing business on the Net is advertising. People are placing ads on Web sites for the very same reason that they place them in print media and on television. They place them there because they want a particular audience to see their advertisement and take action. Popular Web sites, like Yahoo, generate advertising revenue from a wide range of advertisers.

Some people are making money on the Web by providing Web services. Some of these people are consultants, others are Web page designers, others are companies that provide special services using the Web. First Virtual Holdings, for example, provides a service to help businesses conduct secure transactions over the Web. Dealernet (http:/www.dealernet.com) links the home pages of auto dealers to each other. Dealers in more than 20 states utilize this service and pay Dealernet for the privilege.

Another business model is cost-savings. The Net and the Web allow many companies to automate several of their information-sharing and customer-service activities at a dramatic savings. Novell, for example, uses its Web site (http://www.novell.com) to distribute marketing, advertising and customer-service information at a dramatic savings over direct mail.

Finally, many companies are using the Net and the Web to enhance other operations. These companies' primary business activities happen in the physical world, but their effectiveness and efficiency are enhanced by activities on the World Wide Web and the Net. For example, Ragu spaghetti sauce has one of the most popular sites on the

World Wide Web (http://www.eat.com). Ragu builds it around the character of an Italian mother who's a great cook. That character is carried throughout the site. In addition, the site incorporates activities such as contests, recipes and more.

Does Ragu sell spaghetti sauce on the Web site? No. But the site helps the company sell spaghetti sauce in the supermarket by being memorable. People who regularly visit the Ragu site find it almost impossible to walk through the spaghetti sauce section of their supermarket without thinking about Ragu. And that means they're more likely to buy Ragu.

Those kinds of enhancements aren't available just to people who sell consumer products. IBM sells many products to industrial customers. Those customers will gather information about IBM's products by visiting a Web site. This site makes it easy for them to gather information when and as they need it. A purchasing agent will often make several visits to the IBM site for information gathering. But when he or she is ready to purchase, the customer will place a call to or visit the local IBM sales office.

Let's look at one more example. One consultant we know uses a Web site as part of her marketing strategy. The site functions as a 24-hour sales office. Visitors to the site gather information whenever they choose, but the consultant, Suzanne Vaughn, also uses the site as part of her direct sales strategy. Often when she's talking to clients on the phone, she'll have them bring up her Web site. Then she'll walk them through the material on the site point by point as it relates to her sales efforts. She's found this to be a very effective way to enhance her telephone sales.

Direct sales

By "direct sales," we're talking about actually selling a product online: taking the orders and, in some cases, actually fulfilling orders online. If you're considering direct sales as a model you'll use, there are three significant issues that you'll need to address. Those issues are fulfillment, security and ease of ordering.

"Fulfillment" here refers to the process of processing an order and getting the merchandise ordered to the buyer. If you're already filling orders that you receive in other ways, your primary challenge will be to connect your online order-taking to your other fulfillment process.

In many cases this means addressing the issue of forms- and order-processing. Larger companies will usually use their own in-house staff to develop the forms and data connections necessary for order-processing. Smaller companies that use the Web for sales transactions usually find it necessary to use outside help to perform such functions.

Give some attention to how you'll integrate the actual order that you take over the Net or the Web into your existing order-processing system. The more that you can integrate and automate the process, the better it will be. If you use an outside fulfillment service, you might want to have the orders you take online sent directly to the fulfillment service. If you handle the orders yourself, you may want to ensure that any order form you use online matches up well with the order forms you use for your other processing.

What if you don't fulfill orders right now? Consider the case of one of our clients, a specialty retailer. The company's specialty is buying up entire lots of closed-out merchandise and transporting them to stores located in lower-income neighborhoods. When we considered whether this company should conduct direct sales online, we decided we had to build on the company's core competence: purchasing and transportation to a limited number of sites.

We also had to address the fact that the company did not have a fulfillment mechanism for direct orders. All of their orders were handled through their retail stores. In that case, what we chose to do was locate the fulfillment activity at one of the company's regular warehouses. For new online orders, we decided to use the company's own people and a modification of its current shipping system. We established a trial period of six months.

If the experiment with direct sales proves successful, then we'll engage a regular order-fulfillment service or continue to provide that service from the company's own warehouse. The point is that fulfillment is a part of direct sales—one that's often missed by people planning online sales. They also fail to incorporate the costs for fulfillment into their overall business planning.

Security is another issue you'll need to face. There are really two issues here: perceived security issues and actual security issues. Let's take the latter first.

The popular press has been filled with articles about crafty hackers stealing credit card numbers as they fly across the Internet. There have been articles about sophisticated "sniffing" programs that find credit card numbers and capture them. In reality, this type of crime requires a great deal of sophistication on the part of would-be hackers. In addition, people with the sophistication to pull this off will look for sites with a large number of credit cards, not individual sites carrying a limited number.

If you're considering taking orders online—and especially if you'll allow people to use credit cards—you'll need to provide a reasonable level of security. For most business people, this means you'll need to hook up with somebody who understands computer security and how to make it work effectively. If you're a large company, those people will either be in your IS department or they'll know how to find them. If you're a smaller company, consider linking up with one of several companies whose business is ensuring secure transactions over the Net.

There are three basic methods being developed to provide secure transactions. Secure server technology uses encryption to make sure that information the buyer enters is transmitted to the seller so that people who might want to read it won't be able to. Netscape communications is one of the leaders in this area of security. To use this technology, a buyer must order from a seller who is using a secure system.

"Third party verification" systems are those in which a third party verifies that the buyer is who the buyer says he or she is, that the credit card number offered is valid and that the merchant is the person who the merchant says he or she is. The leading third party verification system is probably First Virtual Holdings. To use this sort of system, a buyer registers with the third party and then uses the ID they receive on all transactions with merchants who also work with the verifier.

And there are digital cash systems. With these systems, a buyer pays for a number of what are essentially digital IOUs and then uses them to pay for purchases with participating online merchants. An early entrant in this area is DigiCash. The first bank to set up a way for folks to use DigiCash with online purchases was Mark Twain Bankshares in St. Louis. As with third party verification, both buyer and seller need to use the system.

Of course, if you're doing business-to-business selling, you'll probably be on a purchase order/invoice system anyway. Credit cards will be irrelevant. In that case, the same kind of system that you have for verifying the identity of a buyer and for checking the company's credit will also work for orders that you take over the Net.

But back to credit cards for a moment. How big is your customers' risk of having their credit cards stolen if they order with them over the Net? Actually, it appears to be pretty small. In fact, you're probably more at risk using your credit card in a local restaurant than you are using it over the Net.

Consider this case in point. The Internet Society is made up of people sophisticated about the Net, computers and what's possible on them. The Internet Society handles registration for its conferences online. Members of the society routinely pay for their registrations using their credit cards, and credit card orders are placed using unencrypted electronic mail. Does that tell you something?

But a key point here is that there is a major difference between the reality of security threats online and the perception of them by members of your buying public. For that reason, you'll need to make your customers as comfortable as possible buying online if you want them to do it. Here are some suggestions.

First, provide a secure transaction system. Second, offer alternative ways of ordering. In addition to using credit cards over the Net, give people the option of ordering by phone or by mail. People who are nervous about ordering on the Net may still want to use the Net to put their order together.

Let's take an example: The Covey Leadership Center sells book and tape programs developed by Steven Covey through its World Wide Web site. A visitor can put together an order form that includes several different products. But the order is not actually placed online. Instead, the customer calls, writes or places a fax to the company, providing credit card or other payment information.

If you're not expecting many orders, consider a third option of having people place an order online which you will call them to verify, at which time you will take their credit card number. A similar option used by several people is to put the order itself into two messages. The first of these is the order complete with credit card number. The second consists only of the expiration date of the credit card.

All of these discussions of security and the comfort level of people who may buy from you online bring us to the issue of ease of ordering online. Online, just like with any other kind of business, you want to make it as easy as possible for people to order.

Make it possible for them to get as much information online as they might possibly need. Doing so makes it easy for them to make the full buying decision without leaving your site. It also increases the odds that they will order during a visit to your site.

Make sure your order forms are easy to use and understandable. A trick that's worked for one of the authors of this book is what he calls the "intelligent 15-year-old" test. This test involves checking out your forms, copy and any other aspects with a relatively intelligent 15-year-old.

Generally, 15-year-olds have reading and comprehension skills comparable to the rest of the population, but they're also fearless in telling you what they think doesn't work. Get feedback from sources like this. And don't forget to test your forms out on people like those you could be selling to.

Direct sales can be an effective model for doing business online, but as with many other areas of business, it pays to concentrate on the details and make sure they all work.

Subscription

Subscription as an online business model involves generating revenue from people in a special group, often called members or subscribers. These people get services not available to others. Think of a magazine subscription. Subscribers receive the magazine and non-subscribers do not. Online, there may be several different levels of subscription or membership. One association that we've worked with, for example, offers three levels of involvement and information.

The first level offers information available to anyone who comes to the association's site on the World Wide Web. No special membership or fees are required. The second level, available only to members of the association, offers additional information available from association files. Finally, a subscription service is available for a fee to members of the association. It allows access to several special files and requires a password for access.

One site which uses a similar system on the World Wide Web is the search tool InfoSeek. InfoSeek has certain areas which anyone with a Web browser can use. Other services and searches are available for a modest fee. And it offers a subscription service with significant benefits for people who use search tools a great deal.

Subscriptions are also common with newspapers and magazines. The *San Jose Mercury News* is one such newspaper. At its site on the World Wide Web, the *Mercury News* provides information available to anyone. In addition, there's additional information, including backgrounds on stories, available only to *San Jose Mercury News Online* subscribers. In addition, the *Mercury News* provides a news clipping service, called News Hound, available by separate subscription and handled by electronic mail.

Up until now, we've really focused on Web site applications. But that's not the only way to use the subscription model to make money. You can also generate revenue from subscriptions to a mailing list much in the same way you would generate newsletter subscriptions.

The authors are partners and managers of a Web site for speakers, trainers and consultants (It's at http://www.expertcenter.com). Members of the Expertise Center (the site's name) purchase Web service and marketing support help. The Expertise Center also offers an additional benefit, a mailing list where only members can discuss issues about speaker-, trainer-, consultant- or writer-marketing on the Net and the Web. The Expertise Center follows the subscription membership model we've outlined above.

If you're looking at using this model to generate income, there are two specific issues you'll need to be careful of. The first issue is "gating," how you restrict access; the second is determining which parts of your service are public and which are private.

There are three basic ways to control access to your material. The first, and most obvious, way is simply restricting who you send material to if you're using a mailing list or another e-mail delivery tool.

A second way is membership checking. Most systems can be arranged to do this for you: to determine membership by the e-mail address of the person coming to the site or requesting information.

And the third way is password protection. People would either get or be assigned a password, and that password would be necessary to pass through the gate to where the information is.

The issue of which material is public and which is private, or re-stricted, is a bit stickier. In an information-rich environment such as the Net and the Web, the best way to sell a product is to share information about it. On the other hand, some of that information may be the very information you want to charge for.

The economics of the Net and the Web make it easier for you to charge lower prices for information products than you might have charged before. Let's take a newsletter, for example. The economics of newsletter publishing in a paper world are pretty simple. You need to send out lots of solicitations for subscriptions, and you're best off with a higher newsletter price than with a lower one.

In the digital world, things are quite different. Because your marginal cost of adding a subscriber is pretty much limited to the subscription processing costs and there's no additional cost for producing a digital newsletter issue relative to the number of subscribers, a newsletter can be profitable almost as soon as it's set up. Even limited subscription numbers put you in the black.

A technique that several subscription magazines and newsletters use to both strut their stuff and give subscribers the benefit is to use a sample edition of the electronic publication as a sales tool but with the content either a composite (made up from several earlier issues) or a slightly-dated version of the information.

One of the authors who publishes an electronic newsletter has used both strategies. A composite newsletter has been made available through an autoresponder, and a sample of the newsletter has been available on the Web site. The edition on the Web site is two months older than the current issue.

You might also decide, as InfoSeek has done, that you can provide "piece meal" availability of some of your subscriber benefits on a charge-per-use basis.

Advertising

Advertising as a business model works for those sites and/or services that are so popular that they draw large numbers of people or a specific group of people. That makes them attractive to advertisers in the same way that advertisers are attracted to print and other electronic media.

For example, several of the most popular sites on the Web, such as the Yahoo and InfoSeek search tools, now have advertisements on them. In both cases, advertisers pay to have their message, which includes a link to their site, on the popular search tools.

Consider advertising as part of your revenue strategy if you generate a site, mailing list or other service that is so popular it draws folks that other people would want to reach. Then you'll need to set rates for your service.

In the physical world, there are standard methods for determining advertising rates. People selling advertising can point to studies from such groups as the Audit Bureau of Circulation (ABC) to verify how many people are being reached by an ad and what kind of people they are. None of that exists yet for the World Wide Web. Several firms, including the ABC and Nielsen Media Research are working to set up systems that measure how many and which people show up at a particular Web site.

What they are aiming for is something equivalent to the demographic and other information you can get from any other advertising medium. If you want to place an ad in your local paper, for example, the paper can give you information about who its subscribers are. But determining who'll see an ad is, of course, trickier on the Web because while we know who subscribes, we very often do not know who visits our Web site.

If you're considering setting up your site as a place to sell advertising, you'll need to check into the audience measurement instruments are currently being developed by people like Arbitron, Nielsen and Ipro. You might also consider some other ways for documenting the kinds of visitors who come to your site.

Magazines such as *Wired* have used a system in which folks visiting its hotwired site must register and share information about themselves. That information, in turn, becomes part of a database *Wired* can share with potential advertisers.

Other sites gather this sort of information at a point where people get some particular benefit. For example, a visitor might be offered the option to download an information file or piece of software but first must share information about him- or herself.

An emerging issue as the Web gets to be more popular for commerce is the way that Web site operators gather information about visitors. Firms are really trying to keep information-gathering as unobtrusive and well-intentioned as possible. Several companies, such as the publisher CMP and MasterLock, have set up registration processes in which registration is optional. In other words, a visitor is asked to register, but can view information on the Web site without doing so. Watch for information-gathering to become a battle ground between privacy advocates and business folk.

In addition to formal ads that look very much like the newspaper or magazine ads you're used to, another form of advertising on the Net is through paid links. These are situations in which links from one site are paid for by the people at the site being linked to.

An excellent example of this is the Meetings Industry Mall. This is a service site set up for people in the meetings industry. Vendors with Web sites can be listed for a modest fee on the Meetings Industry Mall with links to their sites. The link is paid for, usually, on a monthly basis. Several firms are trying to develop ways to have the link paid for based on the number of people who use it. And you can probably expect that sort of thing to appear within the next year or so. Increasingly we're seeing developments of sites like this with specialty links for people within a particular industry or interested in a particular subject. If you collect large amounts of information that would draw people to your site, consider advertising either with ads or paid links.

Services

If you develop an expertise doing business on the Net, you may find you have expertise that you can sell. People generating revenue through Web sites are doing so by designing Web sites and World Wide Web pages, functioning as consultants, etc. Right now the people generating revenue are those who provide direct services and consulting to people who want to set up shop on the Net and the World Wide Web. Some companies will inevitably develop expertise in setting themselves up and then turn around and market those services to others. You can also expect that there will be, in larger companies, some sort of internal accounting for many of these services.

Cost cutting

All the hype about the Net and the Web as a place for business has focused on the revenue side, especially sales and marketing. But probably the largest effects on the bottom line have come from organizations who have used the Web to reduce expenses.

Expense reduction is especially attractive because the cost of setting up a Web site is relatively low compared to other pervasive ways to do some of the same kinds of information-sharing. Generally the Web can cut your expenses if it can help you automate information-sharing, ordering or any other labor-intensive service.

Eventually, if you look for those places in your business in which someone either spends a good deal of time on the phone with customers/prospects or must in some way fold two pieces of paper, stick them in an envelope, address the envelope, stamp it and mail it, you'll find ways the Web can help you reduce costs.

Think about this. Both Federal Express and United Parcel Service provide services on Web sites that offer customers the opportunity to track packages. In our experience, count on about three minutes to sign onto the Web, get to the Federal Express site, enter the package tracking number and get information back. Now, that's generally less time than we spend making the call to an 800-number, being on hold and getting the information. There are some additional benefits to us as customers as well.

First, the information we get when we track our package on the Web is in printed form and fully-detailed. Basically, it's what a customer service rep at Federal Express would be looking at on his or her screen when we call in. So we've got full information in a form we can share with others—that's a tremendous benefit for us and a market edge for Federal Express. But this improved service is not even the key benefit: Fed Ex and UPS ultimately reduce the cost of package tracking by reducing the time folks spend time on the phone giving out information.

You probably have business functions you can redesign to use the Web and cut costs. In Federal Express' case, the information customers are allowed to have is already available from Federal Express' computer. In addition, the ability to call it up is already clearly defined. All that's left is to deal with security issues and notify customers that the information is available. In an operation in which personnel costs be 60 to 70 percent of expenses, automating significant amounts of a basic function can be a major benefit. The Web can be a great place to do that.

Let's look at another example. A company with which one of the authors has worked has moved toward an online ordering system. This company already has a direct sales operation utilizing an 800-number. The cost for handling an order through the 800-number is about $15 per order. The major portion of that cost comes from the labor involved in order-taking and order-entry. On the Web those costs vaporize. Orders are essentially placed directly by customers who enter their own information. The orders are transmitted directly and almost instantly for fulfillment. And the cost to our client is about $4 rather than the $15 for a phone order.

As you consider the different ways to generate revenue using the Web, also consider ways to reduce expenses. But don't stop there.

Enhancing other operations

For many companies, one of the most effective models for using the Internet and the World Wide Web is to use the information-sharing as relationship-building opportunities. Recently an industrial buyer was looking for laptop computers. This company was prepared to place a substantial order and had been considering one particular vendor.

The company's purchasing agent used the Web as a way to gather information and came upon a site set up by the IBM Corporation to market its Thinkpad product. The purchasing agent used the site to gather information and returned to it several times. Then, when the decision had been made to go with IBM, the agent placed a call to the local representative to place the order.

This is a great example of an enhancement strategy. Because information on the Web is available 24 hours a day, seven days a week, and because the purchasing agent could visit at leisure, the Web became a way to share information without direct involvement from the sales force.

That's really what enhancement is all about—using the power of the tools available to you online to make processes more effective and profitable.

Consider all the models we've mentioned so far. To be effective on the Net and the Web, mix and match approaches to suit your own business and strategic purpose. Keep checking on new options available for modifying and enhancing your processes from there.

Basic strategies

At this point you know about the technologies available on the Net and the Web; we've also covered some of the tools. And you have a decent idea of how you might use the Net and the Web to generate revenues and reduce costs. There's one more step before we move to looking at how specific business functions can be handled on the Net and the Web: core principles for doing business online.

We refer to these as the *Five I's* of doing business online. The Five I's represent specific principles you'll want to follow when developing your own strategies for using the Net and the Web. The Five I's are *Information, Interaction, Individuality, Interest* and *Integration*.

Information

The Net and the Web are information-based media. While options for pictures and sound certainly exist on the World Wide Web, it's still primarily a place to share a dense amount of information. Successful businesses pick up on this propensity for information.

You'll be effective with your online business if you can provide information that's of value to your customers, prospects and friends. Evaluate the value of your information based on how up-to-date and relevant it is. How fresh is the information you have to offer? Does it provide something new for your clients, prospects and friends?

And does it meet the particular needs of the people you're trying to reach? Several Net and Web business people have set up separate sites or separate Web pages and separate mailing lists for different subgroups. This is niche marketing carried to a powerful and profitable extreme.

If you can provide up-to-date and relevant information to the people you want to reach, they will increasingly come to you for that information and for other things you have to offer, such as your products and services.

- - - - - - - -

Interaction

One of the powerful features of the World Wide Web is its ability to set up interactive opportunities for people who visit your Web site. The principle you'll want to follow here is to give people lots of things to do. Direct marketers have known for years that people build involvement by taking actions. That's why several sophisticated mailing packages, for example, have you move a stamp from one place in the mailing package to another.

Giving people things to do also helps them feel in control of the situation. And several marketing studies conducted over a number of years point to the fact that people are more satisfied and more likely to buy in situations in which they feel they have control.

Interaction helps in both of these ways. It helps in another way as well. Having people act in several ways builds their involvement with you and ultimately builds a relationship and community. We'll talk several times in this book about the power of community and the particular ways you can build it online. But increasing interaction is one of the most productive things you can do to build your business.

Individuality

The principle of individuality suggests that all individuals be able to do business with you on the Net and achieve their own solutions in their own way and on their own time. Of course, the Information you've chosen and the way you've set up Interaction will also help people reach individual solutions.

Some factors of individuality are helped by the very character of the Net and the Web. Mailing lists, newsgroups and Web sites are available 24 hours a day and seven days a week. That means that they're available whenever your customers, prospects or friends are interested in checking them out.

They'll also find that if the information is where they can get it easily, they will not need to store it. For that reason they'll come back to your site frequently (as we've found in several analyses of online transactions).

As you design your business strategies, think about ways you can encourage as much individuality as possible. Think about ways to define individual needs and then meet those needs through the technologies available on the Net and the Web. Think about the old marketing line about "finding a need and filling it." We'd modify that somewhat if you're doing business on the Web: "Find a niche (or two or three) and fill it (or them)."

Interest

Because business on the Net and the Web is based on the idea that people will be coming to you rather than you going to them, most of the marketing issues you thought you'd have to address are already defined by your customers, prospects and friends.

The first aspect of making things interesting is to know your audience well. Now this is an old marketing principle, for sure, but it has special application on the Web, where you can tailor information sources so people can tap into their individual or niche needs.

Creating interest has another aspect as well. You may not have thought about this before, but *interaction* is a way to make things interesting. We know, for example, that people who rate conversations as "highly interesting" tend to remember best what they said rather than what their partner said. We also know that having the ability to explore makes things interesting for people.

To the other three I's we've talked about so far, add *interesting* as one of your principles. To find out what interesting is, pay close attention to the people you're trying to reach. Here's how to do that: Ask your salespeople or the people who answer the phones the first questions that people ask when they call. Using some of the tracking and reporting programs available, monitor which parts of your Web site get the greatest traffic. This will give you an idea of what is interesting to your customers.

And you can design your Web site so that people are requesting information. Keep track of what information is most requested, and that may tell you something about what is most important to your visitors.

Integration

Without intending a pun, integration is the place where it all comes together. Whatever principles and whatever models you choose to follow for your Net and Web business, these need to be integrated with your overall business purpose.

That means that your strategies on the Net and the Web will need to match your strategies for the rest of your business. You'll want to build on your strengths while you make your weaknesses irrelevant. Before setting up a business on the Web separate from your regular business, do an analysis of what you do well and find ways to use the Web to enhance that while adding new strategic strengths the Web makes possible.

One clothing discounter in the Northeast was considering setting up a separate Web business. When they analyzed the strengths of their current business operations, they found two things. The first strength was the physical location of their stores in communities where low price but high-quality goods sold well. The other strength was the company's ability to purchase clothes or goods at a deep discount.

As they analyzed their strengths, they determined that the physical location was not the strength they could continue to use on the Web. Further, their customers were not likely to be the sort who would have computers and connections to the Internet. On the other hand, buying close-outs at deep discount was a strength that would lend itself to a Web strategy. The company is now developing a Web site that sells close-out merchandise for a limited period of time. While it's different from their current business, it's still a business that builds on one of their core strengths.

Integration also implies that your printed material refer to your Web sites and e-mail address along with your other contact information. And it implies that your online activities mesh with your other activities.

Consider what the makers of Jeep have done, for example. Full page ads in *The Wall Street Journal* include references to Jeep's Web site. Visitors to the site can gather more information and engage in interactive options that help them learn about Jeep and Jeep's special offers.

Also, Jeep's artwork is similar in the print and the online media. Following the principle of integration in your strategy means that your materials should look similar on the Web and in print. Use logos and slogans consistently so people will have an idea of who they're dealing with regardless of *where* they are when they are encountering your information.

The Five I's of doing business online are the five principles with which you should use your Web business models and Web tools to be effective. In the next few chapters, we'll talk about how you'll apply these principles, models and tools to specific business situations.

Chapter 4

Marketing

Key points

- Marketing is still marketing, but we're not in Kansas anymore: we're in cyberspace.

- Many components of successful marketing are also necessary for marketing in cyberspace.

- In both marketing environments people move along an involvement scale from: 1) ignorance 2) to recognition 3) to awareness 4) to interest 5) to involvement.

- When they've never heard of you, move them to recognition by increasing frequency of contact: integrate your efforts and be present wherever prospects and customers can be found.

- From recognition on, help people buy from you by providing them with as much information as possible—information they can get to easily when they choose.

- Do detailed product and audience analysis when marketing in cyberspace; identify key customer/prospect benefits and use these as entry points to your Web site.

- Design paths through your Web site by asking, "What do we want them to do next?" and "How can we help them do it easily?"

- An autoresponder system can help people get information easily.

- A good marketing strategy uses Net and Web tools to build a community of customers, prospects and friends around your company and what you offer.

- Use newsgroup/forum participation to find out what your customers need and want.

- Use your Web site, newsgroup participation and mailing lists to test your ideas about what your customers want.

- Use the Web to check on your competition.

- Conduct market research online with surveys, questions and focus groups.

- People find your Web site in three ways: using search utilities, through links from other sites and because you direct them there.

- Effective registration tactics improve the odds that people find you.

- Consider using both paid and free links to help people find you.

- Your ads, printed materials and people should direct prospects to your site.

If you've followed any of the many articles on the Internet, you may have come to believe that the World Wide Web is the ultimate marketing medium. There are articles that would have you believe that this particular medium will make you a fortune with minimum investment in either knowledge or equipment. There are articles that try to convince you that marketing on the Internet is quite different from marketing elsewhere because of the constant change in technology. Some of that's true. But marketing is still marketing.

We're not in Kansas anymore—we're in cyberspace

Marketing is marketing because people are still people. They still make decisions in basically the same ways. They still make buying decisions primarily emotionally and then rationalize them intellectually. People still need a while to become comfortable enough with a business to do business with it.

Many components of successful marketing are also necessary for marketing in cyberspace. Sure, there are some differences. We'll get to those soon. But the key underlying fact about marketing on the Net is that marketing is still marketing because people are still people.

Let's take a look at how the basic marketing process both changes and stays the same when we move it onto the Net and the Web.

The involvement scale

Many years ago, one of the authors discovered a concept called the "involvement scale" that accurately describes how people move toward a buying decision. The involvement scale includes five stages that work like this.

1. People begin *ignorant*—ignorant of you and what you do. They may even be ignorant that there are businesses like yours.

2. Ideally, they move from ignorance to *recognition*. At this point on the scale, a little bell goes off in their heads when they hear your name or when they hear about the kind of business you have.

3. From recognition they move to *awareness*. At the awareness stage, people not only recognize your name but also know a bit about what you do and maybe even what benefits you might offer them.

4. The next stage along the continuum is the *interest* stage. Here people begin to take steps to consider purchasing your product or service.

5. Once they've considered the purchase, they've moved to the *involvement* stage.

Ignorance	Recognition	Awareness	Interest	Involvement

The marketing challenge is different at each stage of the involvement scale. When people are at Stage 1, the *ignorance* end of the scale, the marketer's primary job is to move them to Stage 2, recognition. In traditional marketing, improving recognition means increasing frequency of contact. And all the weapons in the arsenal are used. Ads are placed in different media. The frequency of the ads is regulated. There are sales calls, brochures and even (as a student of mine put it years ago) "sky writing and stained glass windows."

The same challenge faces you as a marketer on the Net or the Web. Only the tools are different. And you need to make sure your marketing efforts are integrated so the possibility of contact increases.

For example, put the URL for your Web site on your stationery and business cards. Mention it in your print and electronic ads. Include it on the advertising specialties that you distribute.

On the Net or the Web, you'll want to be present in lots of different forums and newsgroups. You may want multiple pages on your Web site indexed through search utilities in different ways. Set your indexing up based on the kinds of words people use to describe their problems, opportunities or interests.

When people are at Stage 2, *recognition,* your challenge as a marketer is to move them to Stage 3, *awareness,* where they'll know more about you and what you do. Again, you'd have basically the same kind of challenge in traditional marketing. And again, your major strategy is to increase the frequency of potential contacts to get people to understand you and your product or service.

When you're on the Net and the Web, however, you'll usually do this by increasing the amount of information people can get about you. Make your Web site as interesting as possible to bring them back several times. And when they return, show them lots of different things to interest them and help bring them back.

As people move from Stage 3, awareness, to Stage 4, *interest,* the quality of their contact with you becomes increasingly important. In general, as people move up the involvement scale from ignorance to involvement, quality of contact becomes more important and frequency of contact becomes (slightly) less important.

So the parts of your online marketing which are permanent, like your Web site, need to be rich with information, interest and benefit for the people you want to reach.

Let's stop here for a minute and underscore another point. When you're marketing on the Net and the Web, you'll need to do the same kinds of customer and product analyses that you do with traditional marketing. Here are some questions you should be asking.

- Who are we trying to reach?
- What do we want them to do?
- Why should they?
- How can we make doing this easy for them?
- What product features really matter to our customers?
- What are the key benefits?

Let's apply these to Web site design. You'll do that careful analysis of the customer or potential customer. You'll probably do a features and benefits analysis just like you would with any other kind of marketing medium. But some things you'll do differently.

For cybermarketing start by brainstorming a list of potential buyer interests along with questions they'd want answered and problems they'd want solved. Your list forms the basis for entry points on your Web site. Each key interest area, question or problem should be an entry point—a page on your Web site should probably be devoted to it.

Assume that people will use these points (provided you've registered the pages correctly) as entry points to your site. Now you have to ask some other, basic questions.

- What will they see when they get to this point?
- What do we want them to do next?
- How can we help them do it?

Answering these questions will help you determine what links should come from the pages on which the initial questions or situations are presented. Follow each link in your mind, and in your design, the same way your prospect or customer might follow it. Then the last set of questions again.

Effective marketing sites are often visited several times by prospects and customers. So make each visit interesting, informative and valuable. You'll need to include quite a bit of information so your page is interesting at various levels.

Remember: As people move up the involvement scale from Stage 3, awareness, to Stage 4, interest, the quality of information people get from your Web site is increasingly important. Once people are interested in your product, they'll be looking for specific information. That includes information about product features, delivery, pricing, etc.

Make sure that information is on your Web site. And don't forget to provide the information in lots of different ways. Why?

You'll want to make getting the information people want as easy for them as possible. So give them several options. A well-designed auto responder system can get people files with information they want at a click of a mouse on your Web site. And it can also make information available to those who have only e-mail, which is often the case in some larger organizations in which e-mail is available but Web browsers are not.

Once people have become customers or clients, your challenge as a marketer is to build the relationship with them. You'll do that in a couple of ways. The first and perhaps most obvious way is through your customer service effort. We'll talk about that elsewhere in this book.

Some of the top marketers on the Net and Web today, however, are starting to think in terms of building communities of prospects, customers and friends. This strategy not only moves customers from Stage 4, interest, to Stage 5, *involvement,* it actually extends the involvement scale.

One powerful tool you have in your cyberpower business arsenal is the ability to build community using an Internet mailing list. If you need a refresher on this tool, turn back to Chapter 2. You can set up a mailing list so people who use your product or service can discuss it with one another. This ability to discuss what you offer has lots of benefits for you—only some of them have to do with marketing.

By having customers or prospects participate in a discussion of your product or service, you involve them more completely. You are in fact building a community that revolves around your company and the benefits it offers.

And you'll get lots of good ideas from the users themselves. Some of the best product, application and problem-solving ideas come not from the company's engineering department. They come, instead, from the people actually using the product or service. With a mailing list, you can get that feedback dynamically and quickly.

We choose the mailing list as the medium for this discussion rather than a bulletin board, forum or newsgroup simply because a mailing list is far easier to set up and use. Any of these, however, will work.

Regardless of which tool you use, the principle remains the same: use the electronic medium to increase users' discussion of your product or service. They'll learn from the discussion and build their involvement with you as you build your involvement with them.

In addition, a bulletin board can become a different and no less powerful marketing resource. Your sales people can direct prospects or customers considering your product or service to the bulletin board to ask questions of other users. In this case, bulletin board discussion is like having a whole file of testimonials right at your fingertips.

You'll also build community simply by including lots of valuable information on your Web site. The more valuable information on your site is to the people you want to reach, the more likely they'll try to reach you.

And don't forget that cyberspace is a digital world. Life there moves at the speed of an electron—that's pretty quick. So your response at every level of your marketing effort has to be quick as well. You can use autoresponders and electronic mail as well as your Web site to make sure people can get the information the want when they need it. For example, your Web site can describe various information files that are available and that can be requested by a visitor through clicking on a button. You can then use an autoresponder linked to the button as the way of completing that information transaction. That enables people to get information at the time they want it, delivered directly to their e-mail box.

You can also use your Web site as a mechanism for people to send you e-mail about questions regarding your company and its products or services. Then you can then send them either an individual or an automated response depending on their particular question. Again, you'd probably use e-mail here because it's both fast and inexpensive.

That's an overview of online marketing. In the rest of this chapter, we'll discuss two specific parts of the marketing effort. First, we'll talk about how to do market research on the Net. Second, we'll show you how to draw people to your Web site.

E-mail

Just as with traditional marketing, use market research to better target your marketing efforts and help you develop products most likely to meet the needs of the people in your market. The nature of the Net, though, makes integrating e-mail into your overall marketing efforts easy.

Pick newsgroups or forums in which people likely to be your customers hang out to discuss things that interest them. As part of your market research, watch what they talk about and what their key problems are. Be thinking about how your product or service can help them solve their problems or seize new opportunities.

You'll participate here as well, and your informed participation will be part of your marketing effort as well as part of your market research. Participate helpfully, answering questions whenever you can. Be sure to use a .sig file, as we discussed in Chapter 3 on techniques. Remember that your sig file functions as both letterhead and a miniature billboard.

Participating regularly in forums and newsgroups will provide a continuing flow of leads and inquiries. You'll also learn a lot about what things people are really interested in and, sometimes more importantly, how they think about those things.

Here are some questions to ask yourself as you review forum or newsgroup activity.

- What are my customers' and prospects' key problems?
- What are the benefits they value most?
- What role does price play in their decisions?
- How important are delivery concerns?
- What kind of after-sale service do they want?

As part of your participation in the forum or newsgroup, ask people to clarify statements they've made or opinions they have expressed. If you begin to sense you're on to a problem or opportunity that has real interest for people you want to reach, prepare a short information sheet. The information sheet should give people valuable information about how they (hopefully in conjunction with your product or service) can solve the problem or seize the opportunity. Let folks in your forum or newsgroup know that such a file is available. Make the file available on your Web site. Then watch what happens.

If you're really on to something, you'll get lots of requests for the file. You can also ask people for additional questions at the same time they make their file requests by clicking on an autoresponder button. That way you'll pick up additional questions and comments that will help you make the file—as well as your marketing efforts—better.

You can also test your concept by posting this information file to newsgroup archives or forum libraries. One especially successful strategy is to prepare several slightly differently-focused versions of the file with different titles. Then compare which title generates the most download requests. This is the one most likely to reach your target audience.

Early in your market research process, you'll want to gather lots of background information. You can use database research for that purpose and gather a lot of information quickly and effectively.

First, take a look at the bibliographical databases available through several online services. These range from specialized services like DIALOG to databases—such as the CompuServe Information Network—available on commercial gateways to specialized databases and archives available in spots around the Net or Web.

You can use these sources to gather information from articles that your prospective clients or customers will read. Here's how that might work: Let's say your prospective market is accounting firms. Search for a list of articles published in those journals in the last year. Finally, review those titles for common themes or problems that accounting firms have.

Let's look at another example. If your company manufactures a particular product, you can search all of the articles that have been published within the last year in more than 1,000 business journals and magazines where your type of product is mentioned. You should get a clear idea of both problems and opportunities relative to your product as viewed by its users.

If research is not something you do well, use an information broker. Information brokers are people whose business is ferreting out this kind of information. Their skill is knowing what databases are available and how to search them most effectively. You'll find information brokers in the yellow pages under "Information Brokers." Many information brokers also participate in online forums and newsgroups.

While you're bouncing around the Net and Web trying to find information to help you market, you should also be checking out your competition. Do that with your Web browser using a bookmark or a hot list file that includes all of your key competitors.

A "bookmark" on the Web is just a like a traditional bookmark. It helps you get back to something you've found interesting. With most browsers, you can easily create a bookmark for any site you find interesting. Then the next time you want to visit the site, just go to your bookmark file (sometimes called a "hot list") and click on the site you want to visit.

If your browser lets you set up bookmarks in categories, set up a category or folder for your competition and list all their pages there. Then check those pages frequently to see what they're up to. Make special note of new product offerings or of new ways they present their products or services.

You can use e-mail or your Web site to conduct surveys and even to put together virtual focus groups. There are three easy ways to set up a survey.

1. Create a form on your Web site and ask folks to fill it out.
2. Instead of doing a survey, ask a "Question of the Week." You may want to share the results of each question with others either by e-mail or by sharing it on your site.
3. One creative way to gather information about those who visit a site is to give them a "self-analysis" instrument to fill out.

SRI, a major consulting firm, uses this third approach on its Web site devoted to the SRI system of psychographics called Values and Lifestyles (VALS). Visitors to the site can find out their own VALS type by filling in information about themselves. They get a reading of their VALS type along with some explanatory material. SRI gets more information for its research about the kind of people online.

You won't have the advantage of statistical validity with a Web site survey since you won't be able to "draw a sample." Essentially, you'll get replies from people who visit your Web site—often the very people and kind of people that you want to reach.

Online focus groups are fairly easy as well. Use a focus group to bring together folks from your potential universe of customers to discuss an item of interest to them. Now, to some extent this is probably already happening if there's a forum, or a newsgroup or a mailing list these people frequent regularly, so use a focus group to supplement the information and impressions you're already getting from those sources. Use your insights from forum, newsgroup or mailing list participation to help you determine which issues to address or what questions to ask in a focus group.

You can run a virtual focus group either by having people all online at the same time or by having them discuss the issue you want them to discuss using a mailing list. In both cases you'll solicit the same kinds of discussion you'd have in a face-to-face focus group. There's an additional advantage, as well, in my experience. People from certain racial or ethnic groups conditioned not to participate vigorously in public meeting sessions seem to participate when online.

Drawing people to your Web site

Lots of the techniques we've talked about so far involve the use of your Web site. A key to all of these techniques is getting lots of qualified traffic to your Web site. People can find your Web site three ways: 1) They search the Web for sites of interest; 2) they arrive via a link from another site; 3) You tell them where to look.

Searching for sites of interest

To search the Web for sites of interest, they'll use one of the many search utilities. Yahoo, Lycos, Web Crawler, Infoseek and many others register pages all over the Web and then index them. Users of the Web use one of these search utilities to find pages of interest to them. Here are some tips on making this system work for you.

To be registered on a Web site, you have to do the registering. There are services out there that do it for you, but you'll probably want to make sure that you directly take care of registering for your business' key pages.

You'll probably also want to register all of the pages highly interesting to your customers, clients or friends. Do this because people can come to you from multiple entry points. On the Web these entry points are different pages. In users' heads, entry points are different questions, problems or opportunities.

Register every page that might be a starting point for someone to find your Web site. When you do that, be sure that the key words to be indexed appear at the top of the page (if they're not in the actual title). Indexing systems increasingly concern themselves only with the top portion of various web pages. If you want them to index the key words you've got, put them high on the page.

Be especially careful about the title you put on your page. You may think your corporate name is delightful. But it may not be of compelling interest to your prospects, customers and friends. You can always include your corporate name with the subject of the page in the title area, but you'll probably want some descriptive material in your page title, in addition to the name.

With all the people setting up Web pages, we'll probably see less and less rigorous indexing. We probably will also see charges for registration or for "premium" registration, which would push your page into the first list of successful searches presented to someone using the utility.

An increasingly common Web business focuses on buyer-service sites. These sites include information about and links to several companies. IndustryNet is probably the best example of this kind of site. To get your pages listed on a site like IndustryNet, you often must pay a fee (which would generally come out of the advertising budget).

Arriving via a link from another site

The second way that people find your Web site is through links from other Web sites. These come in two forms: paid and free.

Paid links are becoming increasingly common. Savvy Net marketers know that there are certain incredibly popular Web pages out there. And they know that if people can link from one of these pages to their page, their "hit" rate—is likely to increase. Hit rate reports were the first activity reports developed for businesses on the Web. Many people think that a hit on a Web page is equivalent to a visitor. That's not the case.

Hit rate reports actually count the number of times that the computer that holds the Web site files is asked for a file. A Web page may be one file or may consist of several files. That means it might count for one or several hits. But the problem gets even more complex. Web browsers can elect to view Web sites without looking at the graphics. They'll choose to do that as a way of speeding up their browsing process. But if they do that, there won't be any hits for requests for the graphic files. And, of course, if a single person visits a Web site several times, they will account for many hits.

Hit rate reports, therefore, are not very effective for measuring Web site traffic or visitors. But they can be effective for measuring *relative* activity. For example, you might view the hit count for your site for the weeks before and after you make a change in your pages. Or you might want to view your hit count before and after you mention your Web site in one of your print ads. In either case, your hit count will give you a relative measure of activity and some idea about whether the change is increasing traffic on your site.

There are really two ways of looking at a strategy like this. If your product or service has broad consumer or business appeal, being on a very popular link from a popular site will probably be beneficial. American Airlines, for example, has put a small ad on the incredibly popular Yahoo page. The ad is in fact a link to the American Airlines page. This works for American Airlines because its services appeal to a broad range of people.

Most businesses' services don't. They appeal to a fairly narrowly-focused range of folks, those with a specific and particular need. In these cases, a link from a wildly popular Web site may be a waste of money. Remember that the goal of most of your marketing efforts is to deliver *qualified* prospects and customers, not just lots of prospects.

For that reason you may want to consider a link from a page related to your business in some way. An emerging business on the Web focuses on industry-specific pages whose owners charge for their links. Prices for this service are all over the map, so you'll need to consider each case on its merits. Consider placing a paid link from an industry-specific site in the same way you'd consider placing an ad in an industry-specific directory.

In addition to paid links to your site, there are also free links to your site. These are usually reciprocal. Another business will provide a link from their site to yours and you will reciprocate with a link from your site to theirs.

Two groups of businesses are good candidates for these reciprocal links. The first type includes businesses likely to refer you. In fact, a link between Web pages is very much like an automatic referral. Think of the other businesses that would normally refer business your way. If they have Web sites, approach them about cross-linking your pages. Be careful to pick only those who you are comfortable referring as well.

The second type of businesses that are good candidates for reciprocal links includes other businesses used by the same customers at approximately the same time as they use your product or service. Again, the same rules apply. Make sure that you're cross-linking with people you're comfortable being identified with—because you will be.

Small note: Very often companies want links from their page to other pages as a way of providing increased value to people visiting their own page. A grocery store, for example, might have links to several food-related sites on the World Wide Web, often those that have lots of recipes. Remember that the real purpose for setting up a reciprocal link is to add value to your page, not just to build links.

Telling people where to look

The third way that people find your Web page is that you tell them in some way where it is and what it's about. One way to do this is by mentioning your Web page in your ads. Jeep, for example, includes a mention of its Web site in the full-page ads it has run in major business publications including *The Wall Street Journal*. Sound View Executive Summaries (a service that provides abstracts of books to busy business readers) includes the URL address for its Web site in its ads in airline magazines.

Anytime you've got an advertisement, a brochure or any other piece of paper that shows up in people's hands, refer to your Web page on it. Anytime you run a radio or television ad that reaches the people who might want to find information on your Web site, your URL for the site should appear as part of the ad.

You'll have better luck drawing them to your site if you tell them in the ad why they should go there. You might say, for example, "For more information on this product, see our Web site..." Or you might mention an information file or tip sheet available at the Web site.

And tell people about more than just your Web sites. For example, if you're using an auto responder as part of the way you get information to people, mention the auto responder in your ads as well.

Don't overlook your sales force as a means of delivering information about your Web site. When you set your site up in the first place, have your sales people use the occasion to call on their customers. One technique that works for a couple of our clients is to have their sales-people visit purchasing agents who they know use the Web. The salespeople actually sit down at purchasing agents' machines and find the new business Web site. Then, right there, they add the Web site to that purchasing agent's hot list or bookmark file.

Also, be sure your inside sales people—in fact, anyone who speaks to customers, clients, prospects or friends over the phone—know about the Web site and how to tell people to get there. Consider directing people to the Web site as an alternative to sending them a fax and certainly as an alternative to folding a couple sheets of paper and stuffing them in an envelope.

These are the three ways that people find you on the World Wide Web: using search utilities, through links and through your own efforts. The most effective way for people to find you, from your standpoint, is when you direct them there. The next most effective way is through links from other sites, and in third place are the search utilities. The utilities are great for reaching people that are searching but don't know much about you yet—they're at the ignorance end of the involvement continuum as far as your company in concerned. But search utilities are really unreliable in terms of delivering the most valuable people you want to reach.

A lot of what determines just how effective your Web site will be depends on how aggressively you make the site a part of your overall marketing and business strategy. You cannot just stick a site out there and expect to do magic. You have to make it work. Making it work for you is not difficult, but you do have to pay attention.

In the next couple of chapters we'll look at specific areas of marketing: sales, advertising and public relations.

Here's a tools/applications chart that illustrates some of the points we've made in this chapter:

Tools	Marketing Applications
E-mail	• Stay in touch with others in the marketing effort. • Gather information with e-mail surveys, etc.
World Wide Web	• Share information in interactive form. • Gather information through surveys, Web site usage statistics, etc. • Check out competitors' Web sites.
Autoresponders	• Make information available to people via automatic e-mail.
Mailing Lists, Newsgroups and Forums	• Keep up on key developments in the industry and in marketing. • Network with potential buyers. • Build a community of users, prospects and friends. • Gather information.

Chapter 5

Sales

Key points

- The sales cycle works Web just as it does offline.
- The sales cycle includes prospecting, cultivating, defining needs, presenting solutions and confirming the agreement.
- There are three basic ways to prospect Web. You can use online databases. You can use forums and newsgroups to generate leads. You can scour the Web for folks who might make good prospects.
- You can use Web sites, mailing lists, autoresponders and e-mail as part of your cultivation strategy.
- Clipping services can help you prospect and also provide you with articles to send to prospects as part of your cultivation process.
- The cultivation process includes the deepening of a relationship, and mailing lists are an excellent tool for that.
- Test your perception of needs by producing short articles and getting reactions to them.
- Your Web site should be a place that prospects and customers visit frequently when and as they need.

- Use mailing lists and internal web sites as a way to keep your employees up to speed on organizational successes and good ideas that work in the field.

- Cultivating and presenting solutions often merge in selling on the Net and Web.

- The technology of the Web can make placing orders easy.

- Secure transactions are an issue you'll have to address if you sell to consumers.

- Developments are fast and furious in the area of security.

- Business-to-business sales often bypass the secure transaction issue because they're done through purchase orders and invoicing.

- Consider general and "niche-specific" cybermalls as a tool for online sales.

- Use your Net/Web activity as a way to enhance sales through traditional channels.

With sales, as with marketing in general, you'll do a lot of the same things Web that you do in traditional sales and marketing. Your prospects are the same in either environment. On the Web, though, the technology makes quite a bit of difference in how the presentation is done. The sales cycle has a clearly-defined set of five steps.

1. First there's prospecting: making the effort to find the people or businesses most likely to be profitable and happy customers or clients.

2. That's followed by cultivating for new prospects. This is a process of building the relationship, building a community. For existing clients and customers, it means extending and deepening your relationship.

3. Then there's defining needs. Here you and a prospect define and clarify exactly what problem needs to be solved or what opportunity needs to be seized.

4. Once the need is defined, we move to presenting solutions. At this point you're saying, in effect, here's what we can do for you.

5. And at the end of this cycle is completing the sale or confirming the agreement.

Obviously this brings us back again to the point at which we build relationships that keep individuals and businesses customers for life. We'll handle this issue, along with marketing in general, in the customer service chapter. For now, let's look at the steps in the sales cycle in a bit more detail and talk about how online technology can help you be effective.

As you read through this chapter, think about how your sales process works. Clearly this is a different process if you're selling a physical good at retail to an individual consumer than if you're selling an information product business to business.

Because sales processes vary, make sure you clarify in your own mind how your sales process generally works before you begin looking at ways it will work in the digital world. Remember that people tend to make buying decisions in pretty much the same way Web as they do in offline. They have the same kinds of interests, worries, concerns and aspirations.

You'll find that the online world helps you accelerate parts of your process and automate others. You'll also find that being Web helps you deepen and enrich some aspects of your sales process and your relationships.

Prospecting

There are three basic ways to prospect Web. You can use online databases. You can use forums and newsgroups to generate leads. And you can scour the Web for folks who might make good prospects.

Using online databases

First, you can use available databases. We've talked about this earlier as a marketing strategy, but you can also use online databases to search for particular types of customers or clients. In addition to the databases available through commercial providers, there are also firms that provide special dial-up access to their information systems.

One of the leaders in this area has been American Business Information in Omaha, Neb. You may know them as American Business Lists, one of the largest purveyors of business mailing lists for businesses. You can dial up their computer in Omaha, Neb., and search for just the kinds of business contacts that you need. You can make your selection based on SIC code, number of employees, geographical location and sales volume; and you can download the information right to your computer. That information comes with freshly-updated names, addresses and phone numbers. Quite a deal.

As the world, and business, becomes more digital, you'll find more and more companies making their information services available directly online. Some of these will do it through commercial services; others will set up their own Web sites; and most will use a combination of means to make business information available to you.

Of course, if you sell business information, you could be one of these purveyors.

Using forums and newsgroups

In addition to finding prospects through online databases, you can also generate lots of leads and inquiries through your presence in forums and newsgroups. Here your helpful presence and appropriate mention of what you do and what you have to offer will almost always generate a continuing flow of inquiries about your products and services.

Some of the inquiries you'll get as folks visit your Web site and seek information there. If you use a sig file with your Web site as part of your signature, these visits will happen fairly often. Some of your inquiries and replies will come when people go directly to your auto responder for a file. If your auto responder is mentioned in your messages or in your sig file, people will use it with some frequency. Finally, some people will just make a direct request to you. They'll say something like, "Tell me about what you do." Or they'll say, "Can I get more information about..."

There are a couple of effective ways to respond. First off, make sure you respond in the forum or newsgroup. In most forums or newsgroups, including any two (but not all three) of the following is acceptable: a description of your product or service, a price or ordering information. Acceptable practice varies from newsgroup to newsgroup, however, so you'll want to be sure to check this out for any newsgroup or forum in which you participate.

In any case, when you respond with a message posting, include some information as well as a way to get other information. You'll be most effective if you have an automatic means (such as an auto responder or Web site) and offer the option of personal e-mail.

Your presence, for prospecting purposes, on a newsgroup or forum will be effective to the extent that you are perceived not only as a knowledgeable and helpful business, but also as a knowledgeable and helpful person. Have individual salespeople participating in newsgroups and forums instead of creating just a formal company presence. If it makes most sense from a technical standpoint to have one person handling all of your online presence issues, make sure that's somebody knowledgeable about end-user issues and articulate in an informal, written medium.

The leads you'll pick up from forums and newsgroups are generally pretty good, and they can often be hot. Remember that you're in a digital forum; quick response is important. Somebody should be checking the forums and newsgroups in which your participate at least once a day and preferably more often. If you've got international customers, prospects or friends, check more frequently and check on a schedule that lets you respond promptly to people in very different time zones.

Scouring the Web for prospects

Another way to use the World Wide Web for prospecting is to look for the Web sites of people who might turn into your customers or friends. Search occasionally for individuals or companies that might be customers for you and also for people who might be good strategic alliances: folks who might refer you or folks whose pages you can link with your own.

This doesn't take much time: it should take no more than a few minutes a week. But it can yield big dividends. If you can find powerful strategic alliances that you can link to on the Web, both of you will do better.

Cultivating

As you move to cultivating, consider both active and passive ways to improve your relationship.

The passive ways revolve around the information you have available on Web sites, mailing lists and autoresponders. If you've got good, rich, relevant information, people will continue to look for it. We find that people will often visit a Web site several times before making a buying decision. We also find that the kinds of information they gather at the Web site each time are likely to be very different. Basically, as they move along the involvement continuum and as they move further along in the sales cycle, they'll seek more detailed and more specific information.

Don't forget to include on your site the kind of information that helps people validate their own interests and ultimate buying decision. Testimonials, lists of clients and referral links are all very powerful in helping to cultivate prospects.

Be sure to use e-mail as part of your cultivation process. If you've identified a good prospect and you're moving him or her along in the sales process, one excellent tactic is to find articles of interest to your prospect and send them to him or her via e-mail. You can find articles easily by using one of the clipping services we referred to in Chapter 2. Remember that you can use a clipping service not just to keep up on your own field but also to capture quickly and easily articles of interest to your prospects. Since you've got the article in digital form from your clipping service, just the click of a couple buttons forwards the article to an e-mail list of prospects.

Don't forget to do this with articles about your business, and include positive press. Otherwise, people won't actually see the praise that your company receives. When you receive favorable press, make sure you get an electronic clipping of the story and send it to anyone it will help you cultivate.

The cultivation process includes the deepening of a relationship. Mailing lists are important to this process, but usually they'll work only with folks already customers and prospects for future business. Getting folks to participate in a mailing list if they're not already interested in what you do is difficult.

Defining needs

Nevertheless, your participation in newsgroups and forums and your regular scanning of information sources about your business and your customers' businesses will help you carefully define particular needs. Consider putting together short articles that address your perception of needs and what you see as possible solutions. Make these available as part of the information on your Web site or through autoresponders. Mention them in your newsgroup postings. See what kinds of responses you get and sharpen up your articles and tip sheets from there.

You can also build in quick diagnosis instruments connected to your Web pages. If you've got knowledgeable buyers, consider letting them develop their own price quotes Web. DEC did this with its computers. Potential buyers could develop their own quotes, good for 60 days.

This kind of system is relatively easy to set up. All it takes is hooking up existing information you already have in your company files, perhaps even the kinds of forms that you let your employees use when they prepare quotes. Then, with due attention to security, make that same information available through a Web site or an e-mail form. If you want to do this, be sure to check the system out thoroughly before you take it "live." Give your reps and field salespeople an opportunity to find the problems and offer their suggestions.

A mailing list can be an effective way to keep your salespeople up-to-date on new applications. One of the biggest challenges many companies have, especially companies spread over a wide geographical area, is keeping the salespeople up on what other salespeople are doing and what great ideas work for them.

Part of that problem comes from the difficulty in just gathering stuff and putting it out in paper form. Some editor, in that case, has to decide what is of interest to everyone in a particular sales group. On the other hand, a mailing list using a listserv for your sales and applications people can help these folks share success stories. Then they can use the success stories as part of their cultivation process.

Information-sharing using mailing lists is powerful because it's interactive. A salesperson in one part of the country can post a note about how something worked with his or her particular customer. Another salesperson in a totally different part of the country and maybe even a different part of the company can look at that and zap! it sparks an idea. Because the mailing list is interactive, the second sales person can ask questions or make comments that can get response from the original person as well as from other people with a broad range of knowledge and experience.

Mailing lists are also great tools to keep salespeople, design engineers, customer service people and others inside the company who work on customer solutions sharing ideas and their successes.

Recently, we've seen several large companies using internal Web sites to do this same kind of communication. The IBM Corporation has set up part of its internal Web site for just these purposes. Individual salespeople and application engineers share their successes and present models of what others might do. Those others ask questions and try to help adapt the models to different situations.

This process is exciting because it makes use of the power of a technology that works on a global scale to share information within an organization. Tom Vassos of the IBM software lab in Toronto and a frequent, valued contributor to online forums, describes this as the Intranet, that place where people within the organization use networking and Hyperlink technology to share information, successes, inspiration and ideas. It's a powerful tool you can use as well.

Presenting solutions

In traditional selling, presenting solutions is often a separate and distinct step. On the Net and the Web, it often merges almost indistinguishably with the cultivating and defining needs steps in the sales cycle. What happens here is that the information that helps people define their own needs also presents them with solutions. The same information that tells people you have potential solutions to their problems tells them what those solutions are.

In this powerful medium, the driver is the customer or prospect, their needs and their questions. The solutions and the need statements tend to intertwine with each other and follow each other in swift sequence. Still, there are times when you'll need to present a solution to a prospect, and this process can be enhanced through powerful networking technologies.

Consider using electronic mail as a way to present material. Even if you can't do the formal presentation this way, you can do much of the pre-presentation work: laying the groundwork and outlining specific points. You could also follow up after the formal presentation with both e-mail and paper mail to restate key points and offerings.

Consider preparing material, including your presentation and supporting material, as a set of HTML files. HTML, you'll recall, stands for Hyper Text Markup Language. HTML files are the kind of files used on the World Wide Web and they incorporate the ability to link information.

You can prepare these files and send them via e-mail. Then individuals can view the files on their own computer using the same browser they use to look at the files on the World Wide Web. If the company has an internal Web site, several people can view them.

These files can then be easily placed, along with appropriate graphics, on a customer's computer or internal web site where several decision-makers can get to them when and as they need to.

You could also set up a separate set of pages on a separate site and let the customer know the specific address where these can be found. There are some competitive intelligence issues here, and you will want to consider some of the security implications. But consider, at a minimum, the possibility of using Hyperlink technology as a way to present both stand-alone and supplemental information.

Confirming the agreement or closing the sale

Presenting solutions in the normal sales cycle results in confirming the agreement or closing the sale. Even this last stage of the sales process is possible using the electronic means of the Internet and World Wide Web.

The best way to complete actual sales on the Web is to merge the "interest" and "involvement" stages of the Involvement Scale using technology. Virtual Vineyards has a Web site that does this extremely well. Virtual Vineyards is a business that sells wine and high-quality gourmet foods through a World Wide Web site. The company allows visitors to its Web site to browse through a broad range of selections of wines. For each selection plenty of descriptive information is available. And each selection offers the site visitor the option to indicate that he or she would like to purchase that selection.

The site visitor indicates this by clicking on an "interest box." When the visitor is ready to order, he or she moves to the order form, and *voilà!* there are all the selections which had the interest box checked. At that point the visitor can modify the order form by removing items, modifying quantities, etc. He or she can also return to the information listings on any selection.

The whole process makes shopping easy for the visitor to Virtual Vineyards' site; this shopping ease results in more sales and happier customers.

One of the issues related to the Web and the Net has been the ability of people to make secure transactions. To some extent this issue hearkens back to when credit cards first became a means for placing orders over the telephone. In the beginning, people were quite reluctant to use them. Later that reluctance waned as the amount of risk came to be better understood.

To some extent this evolution will occur with the Net and the World Wide Web. But there are also some real security issues. In the next couple of years, we'll see several ways for people to complete transactions on the Web. Look for three ways they'll be able to make payment. The first will be some kind of direct encryption system. In a system like this, which will enable the use of credit cards Web, a credit card account number or other important transaction number will be encrypted and then sent across the Net. At the other end, the person doing the selling will decode the message and use it to effect payment using the credit or debit card.

There are also likely to be different versions of third party verification payment systems. In a system as this, a third party would sit between buyer and seller. That party would verify that both buyers and sellers are who they say they are. The party in the middle would handle the details of getting the credit card, debit card or bank account number.

And there is another option. We call it "cash." With the two previous payment methods, payment will be liked to an individual buyer. But in the future look for some form of digital cash, a method of payment not linked to an individual buyer. In other words, this digital cash will be transferable from one person to another, used similarly to tokens, and not linked to an individual's credit card or bank account.

Actually, for many business-to-business transactions, there's already a secure method for handling payment arrangements. It's the system of purchase orders and invoices. If your product is being sold to business buyers, this is mostly likely how you'll confirm orders and take payment, bypassing the entire secure transactions issue.

The special case of cybermalls

Perhaps the oldest way businesses have sold things Web is through cybermalls—collections of businesses grouped on the Net for the purpose of selling things. The first of these was probably the CompuServe Mall.

Traditional malls developed as a way to make shopping easier for people by putting lots of different stores in one place. There's usually an anchor store, like a Sears or JCPenney, that draw people who then shop at the other stores as well.

In cyberspace malls also provide ease for shoppers, but in cyberspace this happens either by making the search easier or by making transactions secure or both. The Internet Mall, for example, is organized by "floors," each of which is devoted to a particular kind of merchandise. This helps consumers to more easily view a wider array of offerings and comparison shop.

In some cybermalls, the mall itself handles transactions. That means that a merchant who might not be able to handle an account with a digital cash service can still have secure transactions because the mall has the account. In other cases, the mall is just a way to group descriptions of different businesses, but the businesses handle the transactions themselves.

If your business is considering taking "space" in a cybermall, ask the following questions.

• How many people will find my products at the mall?

• Will they be people who are likely to buy from me?

- What's the cost of being present in a mall versus the cost of alternatives?

- Will being in a mall fit in with my other marketing and sales efforts?

There's an increasing trend in mall-type Web sites toward sites that concentrate on a particular type of product or attract a particular type of buyer. BookStacks, for example, groups several businesses that sell books; The Meeting Place provides links to a variety of businesses that might interest a meeting planner. If you are marketing to an identifiable niche, a mall devoted to that niche could be a great addition to your marketing and sales strategy.

Sales through traditional channels

For most of this chapter, we've concentrated on sales as they happen on the Web and Net; but for many businesses, the Web and the Net serve primarily to enhance more traditional sales channels.

Information on a newsgroup or Web site can direct prospects to phone numbers they can call. Many retailers, such as Wal-Mart, use their Web sites to provide locators that customers can use to find "the store nearest you." Going the other way, field salespeople can direct prospects to a Web site as a 24-hour source of information. All approaches you use should work together.

It's been said that "nothing happens till somebody sells something." Selling on the Web turns that expression almost on its head. On the Web it's "selling can be a part of everything that happens."

In the next chapter we'll look at functions that help set up sales—advertising and public relations—and how to use the Net and Web to do them better.

Here's a tools/applications chart that illustrates some of the points we've made in this chapter:

Tools	Sales Applications
E-mail	• Use sig file to function as a running billboard on all e-mail communications. • Stay in touch with members of the sales team. • Share information. • Use e-mail as part of your contact strategy with customers and prospects. • Forward articles of interest, via e-mail, to customers, prospects and friends.
World Wide Web	• Provide online ordering. • Use Web site to support sales efforts. • Direct purchasing agents and buyers to Web site. • Provide pictures or product demonstrations as well as specifications.
Autoresponders	• Allow those with only e-mail to retrieve product or service information automatically.
Mailing Lists, Newsgroups and Forums	• Keep up on key developments in your industry and in sales work. • Prospect through participation in selected newsgroups, forums and mailing lists.

Chapter 6

Advertising and Public Relations

Key points

- The state of advertising on the Net and Web today is almost exactly that of TV advertising in the early 1950s—using models from older media while developing methods precisely suited to the new medium.

- We have some idea of what works for Web advertising and how it will evolve.

- Advertising on the Net and Web will be content-driven.

- Advertising on the Web will involve multimedia.

- Advertising on the Web will be interactive.

- Advertising on the Web will be based on a model in which the client, prospect or friend comes to you.

- Advertising on the Web will be directed to an upscale consumer.

- Marketing communications on the Web often straddle the line between public relations and advertising.

- Filing news releases electronically makes them available to a wider public at a lower cost than paper/mail filing.

- Newsgroups, forums and mailing lists can be a part of your targeted public relations strategy.

- Learn the rules for using forums and newsgroups by reading the FAQ (Frequently Asked Question) file and by watching how they work.

- Use a Web site as a key part of your "investor relations" efforts and as a way to tell your side with controversial issues.

Learning how to do it right

In the early 1950s when television was just becoming a vibrant part of American life, businesses and advertising agencies were learning about the medium right along with all the rest of us. At the time the ads on television appeared very much as if they were hybrids of other things carried over to a new medium.

Some ads looked much like print ads to which sound had been added. Other ads were radio ads to which someone had added a couple of pictures. They were not, as we can tell now from the vantage point of some 40 years, television ads. Television ads took time to develop.

Advertising is almost exactly at this state right now on the Internet and the World Wide Web. As usage of the Web begins to skyrocket and as business comes pouring onto its digital domains, we're learning how this medium will be used for business purposes, especially advertising and marketing.

Advertising is a peculiar phenomenon in business. John Wanamaker once said, "Half the money I spend on advertising is wasted—I just don't know which half." This is true for lots of folks.

There are two basic kinds of advertising whether on the Web, in print or in electronic media. Image advertising presents the story of the company but does not incorporate any response mechanism that allows a specific and direct counting of the number of people who take positive action because of the advertising. A print ad for an automobile would most likely be image advertising.

There is also direct-response advertising. Here, there is an immediate response mechanism—a prospect can call a special number, mail in a coupon or order form to request more information or actually purchase the product or service. The mail ads you receive for magazine subscriptions are usually direct-response ads.

Both kinds of ads are finding their way onto the World Wide Web. It's an exciting time to be looking at advertising on the Web, but it's also a time of experimentation.

You can expect that for the next several years advertising on the World Wide Web will continue to evolve. You can expect that folks advertising there, including you, will mostly be trying to adapt older models to a new medium. And you can expect that advertisers, including you, will be developing new and exciting ways to use this medium most effectively for advertising.

Even though Web advertising is a developing area, we know some things about how it's likely to evolve. And we can give you some guidelines about how you to use advertising effectively. In general, we'll make five key points about how advertising on the Web works now and is likely to work in the future.

Point 1: Advertising on the Web and the Net will be content-driven. Cyberspace is very much a content, or information, medium. Your advertising there will be effective to the extent that is uses the information capabilities of the medium.

Point 2: Advertising on the Web will be multimedia advertising. The World Wide Web is the first mass medium ever to give us the capability to combine media. While some of this is still in elementary in form, eventually advertising on the Web will utilize text, pictures, sound, video, animation and other forms of multimedia. In fact, we think one of the challenges to Web advertising will be finding ways to capitalize on the Web's multimedia character.

Point 3: Advertising on the Web will be interactive. Up until now, the main medium for interactive advertising or marketing activity has been the face-to-face sales call. But with the World Wide Web, prospects are able to be involved in the advertising itself. A major challenge to advertisers over the next decade or so will be finding ways to fully use this powerful capability. This characteristic of Web advertising will be especially powerful because getting people involved in a process increases their commitment to it. To the extent that Web advertisers and marketers involve people in their advertising message, they will not only have more effective advertising, but build long-term customer commitment as well.

Point 4: Advertising on the Web will be based on a model in which prospect, client or friend will come to you. Until now, common practice has been for advertising to go to the person. That had been true whether it's direct-response advertising that comes to someone in the mail or a newspaper ad that sits waiting patiently on a page of *The Wall Street Journal* for a prospect to turn the page. With the Web, that model shifts. Increasingly we'll expect people to come to a Web page and, in fact, return several times. This behavior changes the game significantly. It means that advertisers can expect more opportunities to share information—if they make that information valuable. But it also means that the high intensity of certain forms of advertising must diminish to make the return visit more comfortable.

Point 5: Finally, advertising on the Web will generally be directed to a more upscale consumer than mass-market advertising. Recent demographic studies tell us that about 14 percent of Americans use the Internet and the World Wide Web. What's really significant, though, is a finding from a study called the Affluent American Study, which determined that 29 percent of those using the Internet and the Web come from households with incomes greater than $100,000. One of the things that sets the Web apart from traditional advertising media is that it is an elite medium. People are more likely to own personal computers, to have computers at work and to utilize those computers if they have higher incomes or educational levels. This elite audience can create a major opportunity for Web advertisers.

Let's look at these five points, or aspects of future Web advertising, in more detail.

Content-driven

Ads on the Web even now are more content-driven than ads in traditional electronic or print media. There are two reasons for that.

First, the medium is an informational medium. The Internet in fact grew up as a way of sharing information among research, governmental and educational sites. Information-sharing was the reason the Net was created. So historically, how people have used the Internet and the World Wide Web has revolved around the informational or content areas of various activities. Even when people advertise on the Net and Web, they usually find it best to provide a great deal of information.

The second reason the Web and the Net are primarily content-driven is simply that few options exist right now for the kinds of visual and sound presentations possible in other media.

Let's take the example of a sound file. In theory, it's possible to have a sound file available on your World Wide Web site. You could have a greeting from the chairman of the board. Or perhaps you might want to include the keynote speech at your last convention. There's a problem, though. It will take longer for that file to be down-loaded to the visitor's computer than it will for him or her to actually hear the sound. And the higher the quality of sound, the larger the file must be and the longer it will take to transfer. The result is that sound and moving visuals are possible on the World Wide Web, but they generally take far too long to use to be practical.

When a viewer loads a World Wide Web page, his or her browser goes after several specific files. Those files can include information, graphics, sound or just about anything. The problem comes because at processing speeds currently available, and with the current level of sophistication of compression technology, the files that would create an impression much like in other media take longer to load than human attention spans can stand.

Right now, loading a file of good quality audio typically takes longer than playing that file back. The same is true, only worse, with video. Sound and video files are huge compared to text files. And human beings will wait only about nine seconds for something to happen before they get bored. So people browsing the Web will wait only about nine seconds for a page to load and show them what's there.

The result has been that advertising on the Web has been more content-focused than it probably will be in the future. Almost every day advances in compression and graphics technologies make it more likely that sound, pictures and video will become more important parts of Web design.

There's another aspect to this as well. The current state of the art of putting up Web pages provides fewer design options than are available for designing print, radio or television ads.

For these two basic reasons, the most effective ads on the Web have turned out to be ads that are strongly informational. Don't count on Web advertising staying this way; the World Wide Web is at its core a multimedia medium.

Multimedia

We're just beginning to see the power of this in advertising on the World Wide Web, but the technology that makes the Web possible also makes it possible for the Web to be a multimedia medium.

In theory, creating a Web page with pictures, video, sound, animation and a host of other effects is possible. This page might be created to be triggered by the arrival of a browser on the page, or by the click of a mouse button. Most of the examples of how these effects can be used are so far pretty crude. But you can bet that as time goes on and the technology advances, you'll see more and more multimedia Web pages that do an effective job of advertising.

Interactive

The World Wide Web has the potential to be an interactive medium. We say "has the potential" because it really isn't yet. True, lots of pages have a certain degree of interactivity. In fact, the very act of clicking on a link and moving to another page is a form of interactivity. But most of this is what we call "static interactivity": the person interacts with a data file or interacts on a very limited basis with the page itself.

For example, on many search pages, someone types in an item to be found and initiates a search by clicking a mouse button or pressing the return key. A database is then queried, and the results are posted. While that's more interactive than, say, a newspaper ad, it's not interactive in the sense that will be possible fairly soon.

Here again, technology is the force controlling creativity. And this of course means that the situation won't be as limited for long. Almost every day, ways are developed for people to interact with a page. In the next year or so, you can expect to see many different ways for a person to visit your Web page and have a live chat with others. With a live chat, people are actually communicating in real time with each other. That already happens in the chat rooms on commercial gateways such as America Online and CompuServe, but it's been fairly limited on the Web.

Once live chat becomes more common, you can expect companies to begin to provide a certain amount of "virtual presence" on their Web sites. That would work something like this: You or one of your customers would visit a Web site where you would have a question that couldn't be answered by the information you find immediately. You then click a button that would summon a real person to a live chat. You'd type a question and get a typed answer from a real person somewhere else in the world.

Several companies have already experimented with virtual presence and found some concerns. For one thing, using a Web site as a means for customer service using virtual presence means the page needs to be staffed 24 hours a day, seven days a week. This is especially important if your product or service has a global market. Naturally, too, you'll want to staff with people who can speak a variety of languages. English may be the "official language" of the World Wide Web, but it certainly isn't its only language. And, of course, the people there to provide advice need to be qualified. If your company offers a broad range of products, people handling the virtual presence part of your Web site need to have expertise in that same broad range.

One way a couple of high-tech firms have experimented with virtual presence is by having experts on call. A customer service expert in a particular product or process would not have to be at the company office; in fact, with the global nature of the Internet, he or she could be just about anywhere in the world where an Internet connection was possible. Then, at a time when somebody needed that person's advice or special expertise, he or she would be called in some way to participate. From there it's just a matter of simply connecting or following an online procedure to connect expert with questioner.

This process, however, turns out to be simple but not easy. Companies considering a virtual presence on the Web will certainly have to consider staffing and expertise issues as they make basic business decisions.

But let's get back to the interactive nature of Web advertising. Most of the time in the current state of the art, "interactive" means giving the visitor to your Web site something to do. Clicking on links is one obvious thing they can do. But there are several others, such as placing an order, requesting a file, reading information, answering a question, filling out a survey or taking a test.

Why bother with interactive techniques? Direct marketers and salespeople have known for years that if you can increase interaction, you increase the likelihood of sales. Many retail salespeople know, for example, that the more questions they ask you that require a response, the higher the likelihood that you will buy something from them. The same is true on Web sites.

A special advantage that the Web offers in this regard the ability to have people interact with the page at many different times and for many different reasons.

They come to you

In traditional advertising, ads are designed with the idea that they'll have only a limited amount of time to work. Consider this example: You come home from work at the end of a long, hard day. You grab the mail from the mailbox. If you're like most folks, you'll stand next to a table or next to the wastebasket and sort your mail—standing. You'll flip through, keeping some stuff to read and sending other stuff directly to the round file (the wastebasket).

The first test a piece of direct mail must pass is to be interesting enough for you to actually sit down and read it. Direct response marketers call that the "sit down" test. Then, it must be good enough to hold your attention from the initial awareness right through to action. Very rarely—very, very rarely—will people save a direct response mailing piece and act on it later.

The same kind of situation occurs with a newspaper print ad. A person thumbing through *The Wall Street Journal* must be stopped by the graphic display of an ad and then enticed enough to absorb its message. Even when this happens, the amount of time spent with an individual ad will be minutes at most and normally seconds or fractions of seconds.

The World Wide Web gives us a whole different way to approach this phenomenon. Because adding lots of information and features to a Web site is easy and not cost-prohibitive, you can provide a wide range of information and a wide range of methods for accessing that information.

Good advertising strategy on the Web, then, revolves around getting people to come back several times as their needs and their questions change. When General Electric first put up its Industrial Product Web site, it included more than 2,000 printed pages of information. Why so much? So that there would be enough information, creatively linked, to bring back visitors again and again for different reasons.

Or consider the Web site run by the 3M Corporation. There an array of information about innovation draws folks back to the site, where they will also (and easily) find information about 3M products.

Effective advertising on the Web differs from other advertising because it can allow people to return time after time to the information and find it different at each visit. This strategy works particularly well because advertising on the World Wide Web is generally aimed at an educated consumer.

Educated consumer

We've already alluded to one study that found that 29 percent of households with income over $100,000 connect to and use the Internet and World Wide Web. But that's not the only study that we have to work with. Other research indicates the following trends. More and more households have personal computers. Right now the penetration of PCs into households is about 35 percent, and that's rising fairly steadily. The penetration of computers into business is already essentially at the saturation point.

More and more computers in households are communication-capable. In fact, in the last few years, household computers quite commonly arrive with a modem and sometimes with software for a commercial online gateway, such as America Online, already installed.

Also, people are buying computers for households that are increasingly multimedia-capable. In other words, they're purchasing machines with CD players. The configuration of those machines makes several other things possible, including the ability to use sound, graphics and video files that come from sources other than their computers, such as the Web.

Now all of this buying of computers and technology takes money. And it turns out that the people buying tend to have more money than those who aren't. In the United States and in most other countries, these people are also more highly educated.

What does this mean for you if you're doing business online? To some extent, the education factor brings together several of the other unique characteristics of advertising on the Web. Educated consumers are more interested in content- and information-driven kinds of advertising. They're generally more likely to be proactive and come to you. They're more likely to have multimedia-capable computers.

If you market a product or service to upscale individuals, the Web is probably a great place for you to be. Merchants such as Lands End, L. L. Bean and Sharper Image are already there selling their wares to those very folks.

Buying advertising online

Let's shift our focus for just a moment. In addition to putting up your own ads, you may want to buy advertising "space" online. In the last year, advertisements have started to appear on highly popular Web pages. These ads function very much like the ads in any other medium. The major difference is that these ads incorporate a link to the advertiser's Web site or to a specialized Web site.

Yahoo, for example, is one of the most popular pages on the Web. An ad for American Airlines on Yahoo incorporates a link to the American Airlines Web site. Why does American Airlines go to Yahoo? For the same reason that American Airlines advertises in *The Wall Street Journal* and many other publications and why it places ads on popular TV shows. When Yahoo sells advertising, it is in the business of audience delivery. And if you're buying advertising online, you're buying the audience that is delivered, in this case, to your Web site. You'll want to buy from entities that offer you the size and type of audience you're looking for.

Public relations

On the Web the line between advertising and public relations seems to blur. Many of the activities that go on that would traditionally be called public relations are viewed as advertising by some people using the Web. For example, a news release is generally considered public relations in the physical world. But it's specifically forbidden as a form of advertising in many newsgroups.

And some activities that might more properly be considered ad strategy, because of placement and other issues, actually fall under the heading of public relations when they move to the Net or the Web.

If you're getting the idea that the advertising and public relations areas of business are becoming one and the same in cyberspace, hold on. This might not be true. Let's return to the basic distinction between public relations and advertising. Advertising, by definition, calls for the paid placement of information. Public relations undertakes activities designed to get people to carry information, and the source need not pay for that process. Both of those happen on the Net and on the Web; what also happens is a kind of hybrid area, newsgroups, which we'll talk about in just a moment.

Public relations practitioners were some of the earliest of the online business folk. For many years now, services like Business Wire and PR Newswire have placed the news releases of their subscribers on news wires that feed newspapers around the country.

In recent years, those news wires have also fed various online services, and, increasingly, news releases have been made available to a wider public.

If your company writes formal news releases, you should definitely consider disseminating them through PR Newswire or Business Wire for several reasons. First, as the cost of these services has dropped, the cost for reaching, for example, a national selection of daily newspapers has dropped too. For many businesses today, sending a release over one of the commercial news wires is less expensive than mailing it to a number of dailys.

Second, if you file your news release electronically, it's far easier for a reporter or editor to use. The material is already in digital form. It can be cut, pasted, clipped, modified and dropped almost directly into a newspaper. This makes it far more likely to be used than material that must be typed by someone and then reviewed for errors and accuracy.

Third, electronic news releases are increasingly put up by the online versions of newspapers as part of its background material.

Newspapers such as *The New York Times*, for example, allow readers of the online edition to gather (at a mouse click) background information on stories. That background information very often consists of news releases, some of which the story is based on and others of which on related matters that have come over the wires. This can result in increased exposure for you and your PR material—more than what you'd get if you used a paper news release and sent it to a newspaper or even if you used an electronic news release picked up only in an individual publication.

Essentially, filing news releases electronically increases both the likelihood that a release will be used and the reach of people who may see it. Simultaneously, electronic filing generally decreases your news release costs.

Newsgroups

Newsgroups are places online where people of common interest get together to discuss that interest. They're called newsgroups when they occur on USENET. When a similar type of function happens on a commercial online service, it's called a forum. We've discussed these in detail elsewhere. You can return to Chapter 2 for more material on newsgroups.

Newsgroups and forums can be a critical part of your public relations strategy. As we discussed in the marketing chapter, if you are present in newsgroups or forums that are frequented by the people you want to hear about you or to buy from you, and if you participate meaningfully and helpfully in those forums, you enhance the reach you may have to the reach of the digital world.

It's newsgroups, though, where the line between advertising and public relations becomes kind of fuzzy. Every newsgroup follows two sets of rules—formal and informal. The first of these is defined by a specific rule set, and you'll usually find it in something called a FAQ (frequently asked questions) file. That file will tell you what's acceptable, what isn't, what sorts of behavior are appropriate and which are not. For many newsgroups, commercial messages are admissible only under certain circumstances. Other newsgroups allow no commercial messages at all.

This is significant because a news release can be considered a commercial message. In other words, what would traditionally come under the heading of free placement comes under the heading of commercial activity in the digital world. For example, in the Internet Marketing newsgroup, you are allowed to place ads if they meet certain conditions. So follow this advice. You'll get lots of good exposure if you participate meaningfully and helpfully in newsgroups. But if you want to use a newsgroup as part of your overall public relations strategy, play by the rules.

First, look at the formal rules. Get the FAQ file. Read it. You'll find out what is appropriate and what is not. That way you'll know whether "commercial" news releases are even allowed on the newsgroups you frequent. If they are, they may be subject to certain rules. For example, the Market-L is a mailing list that caters to online marketers. It allows ads to be placed if they meet certain conditions. The ad must offer something of interest to subscribers of Market-L in their capacity as marketers. This means that a book on online marketing would be entirely appropriate as a news release/ad, but a book on the online world in general probably would not be.

On that mailing list there are also several specific things you must do if you want to place a commercial message. You must include the word ad in the subject line of your message so people checking postings in the mailing list know right away it's a commercial message. And you must accurately state what you're offering in that same subject line.

These rules are not too hard to follow. If you do, using this vehicle to advertise should work well for you.

What about an online newsgroup or forum that forbids ads or commercial activity of any kind? In that case you're left with your signature file (.sig file) as the major way you maintain a commercial presence. Your major activity on the newsgroup, mailing list, or forum will be to be helpful and informative. You may also be able to weave in mentions of what you do to help raise awareness about your products or services. But be careful here because there are rules other than the written ones that may affect you.

In any group of human beings, there are really two sets of rules: the formal and the informal. The FAQ file covers the formal rules. Culture covers the rest. So how do you learn about the culture of a newsgroup, mailing list or forum? You learn by watching. Our advice is to "lurk before you leap." Watch to see what's actually happening and what's appropriate. If you find that commercial activity seems inappropriate culturally in a particular newsgroup, abide by those rules the same way you would by the formal rules. You may feel that's unfair or not the way things ought to be, but how you feel will not affect what you can do in the group or on the mailing list.

If you can't post formal releases in a forum, newsgroup or mailing list, reevaluate whether your presence there actually helps your public relations effort. Your strategy of being helpful and including information in your .sig file may be enough, but check it out.

Investor relations

A public relations field that's really grown in the last few years is that of investor relations. These public relations activities are devoted to keeping investors up to speed on what the corporation is doing. They're also devoted to putting a positive spin on any news that might come out about the company.

Several companies have started using their Web sites and their mailing lists as ways to improve their investor relations. Many firms have put annual reports up on their Web site or made them available in other ways to investors. Schlumberger, for example, includes its quarterly results on the Web site and makes its annual report, financial statements and news releases available both there and via autoresponder. Other firms have made one of the purposes of their Web sites communication with the community—a community that has invested in the company.

If investor relations is something about which you're concerned, by all means, consider this as one of the functions you can perform effectively online. You can provide lots of information about the company as a whole slanted toward the potential investor or the current investor interested in how his or her investment is doing. Coming up with ways to do this doesn't take a lot of creativity.

Many corporations, including General Electric and Chevron, include information about their financial performance and corporate goals on their Web sites.

Supporting controversial activities

Many companies undertake certain controversial activities from time to time. Almost any extraction company (an oil company, a coal company, etc.) finds the very activities it engages often controversial.

One way to use a Web site is to publish your side of those controversial issues. Oil companies are a good example. To many people, oil companies are the prime example of money-hungry corporations willing to despoil the environment. The oil companies, not surprisingly, see things a bit differently. They use their Web sites to describe their activities on behalf of the environment. Chevron, for example, does this and even offers visitors the opportunity to download a "wildlife screen saver." The Mobil Oil Corporation includes an array of environmental news, which includes its own news releases about Mobil's actions to preserve the environment.

What's the bottom line here? It's simply this. Advertising and public relations are a slightly different animal when you go on the Web or on the Net. Even so, they retain their basic character. Advertising is something you pay for because the medium in which you are advertising provides an audience you want to reach. Public relations activities are non-paid-for activities you undertake to enhance or improve your image.

When you move to the Net or Web, however, you also have access to an intermediate level of advertising/PR activity that takes the form commercial announcements and notices undertaken in appropriate places on the Network.

Here's a tools/applications chart that illustrates some of the points we've made in this chapter:

Tools	Advertising & PR Applications
E-mail	• Stay in touch with others in the marketing function. • File news releases. • Use e-mail as part of your contact strategy with editors and others important to your advertising or PR efforts.
World Wide Web	• Post documents on your Web site that support advertising and PR. • Use notices in print and electronic media to point to your web site. • Get feedback on the impression you're making. • Build a content-rich, interactive site to which your prospects and customers want to return. • Use your Web site for investor relations and to tell your side of controversial activities.
Autoresponders	• Allow those with only e-mail to retrieve information automatically
Mailing Lists, Newsgroups and Forums	• Post announcements of new products or services in appropriate newsgroups, forums and mailing lists. • Keep up to date on developments in your industry and in PR/advertising. • Get feedback on the impression you're making.

Chapter 7

Production and Quality Assurance

Key points

- In the best businesses, the various functions and disciplines work together and help one another out.
- Mailing lists and newsgroups are great ways for production folks to keep up with their changing disciplines.
- Support information for production equipment is increasingly available on the Web, making it accessible and up-to-date whenever a production person needs it.
- E-mail is an excellent tool for keeping a widely flung production operation working together.
- Virtual project teams can make quality assurance activities possible even when people are separated by geography and time.
- Virtual project teams can be set up using a mailing list or a real-time meeting online.
- Internal Web sites are an excellent way to share production and quality assurance information.

When the authors of this book started in business, the relationship between production and the other disciplines of the business was very different. Production people were isolated, set off in their factory where they generally did not talk to people in other disciplines, including product development and marketing. People in product development and marketing stayed in their own little spheres complaining about how people in other disciplines didn't really understand what the business was about.

In the last few years business has changed quite a bit in that regard. We've come to understand that in the best businesses, the various functions and disciplines work together and help one another out. We've begun a quest for synergy. A good deal of that has happened under the banner of total quality or quality assurance.

Using powerful communication and information tools available on the Net and the Web are an excellent way to enhance the synergy that different parts and disciplines of a business can create and the communication necessary for effective production and high-quality products.

The Web can be helpful whether the products we're talking about are physical products (stuff that gets shipped to other people in boxes) or whether they are information products like software, or newsletters or reports.

Keeping up

For production people, just like everybody else, one of the hardest parts of business is to keep up with all the changes in their discipline.

Several Net tools can be used to help people keep up and sharpen their particular skills. Several mailing lists and newsgroups are devoted to the disciplines that surround production. In addition, more and more manufacturers of the equipment or software used in production are setting up their own mailing lists, bulletin boards and other information sources as well as specific Web sites designed to help those people responsible for production use their materials effectively.

The Net also provides access to databases, usually best reached through the commercial gateways, where specific searches can be done for articles related to particular projects. For production people this is especially powerful because the online databases contain a far broader array of journals than most people would find on their own.

For people involved in production, probably the most powerful information the Net provides is specific support information provided by people whose equipment and software they're using.

For the actual production process, the major applications of the Net appear to be transferring information back and forth between various people responsible for different production functions. Electronic mail with its ease of use and speed is an excellent medium for sharing information about scheduling, production changes, etc. And files can be attached to e-mail. Files can include spreadsheets, schedules, special software, etc. In effect, electronic mail allows a company to integrate many pieces of the production process and to do it quickly and easily.

Then there are some special applications of the Net in production if we're talking about the production of information products, such as reports. In these cases, the actual production can be done at various sites with the pieces being shared via electronic mail.

Several worldwide companies that develop software have programmers in several time zones. A common practice is for one group of programmers going off work to hand off the work on a new application to a group in another part of the world who's just coming in. This strategy maximizes the benefit of a worldwide operation and improves the speed of production.

Quality assurance

Probably the biggest trend to hit production in the last several years has been a renewed emphasis on total quality or quality assurance. In general, the trend has gone from "quality from inspection" to providing the highest quality products and services possible.

The Net/Web supports this trend in two especially important ways. First, there is the wealth of information on the Net related to quality, quality assurance and total quality. Web sites and mailing lists abound to provide information in this critical area. Several associations have been especially active in providing resources and journals that are accessible electronically.

Second, on the operational front, the Net allows two specific ways to put together virtual project teams that can enhance quality by connecting people across either physical space or time. These techniques are simply an extension of the basic quality circle concept that's so common in most quality assurance efforts. In traditional quality circles (by whatever name), all members of the circle usually work at the same place and time. Net or Web quality circles can include people working at different times and in different places. Electronic circles also allow for the possibility of gathering expert input that can quickly be distributed to all of the members of the circle or team.

There are essentially two ways to put together a virtual team. One way is to set up a mailing list for the group and to let the group participate in the mailing list, with everyone getting a copy of project-related information. The other way is to have the team conduct real-time meetings using an online chat room. Let's look at them both.

Using a mailing list for a virtual team

Once the list is in place, any posting by one member of the group is sent to every other member of the group and received via e-mail. We found that the best way to kick off such a list is to have the designated team leader state the general purpose for the list and lay out what he or she sees as the crucial issues facing the team. From there discussion moves rapidly in the directions that team members take it. These mailing lists can also be used as a form of virtual brainstorming.

Virtual brainstorming has some real advantages over traditional brainstorming. In a typical, traditional brainstorming session, a number of people are brought together in a room. They are presented with a problem or question and asked to come up with ideas for solutions or answers. In the classic form, folks shout out their ideas and suggestions, and these are captured by a facilitator, who writes them on a sheet of paper visible to all. The basic rules of traditional brainstorming include no prejudgment of ideas, and all ideas are acceptable.

Since its development in the early 1950s in the advertising business, brainstorming has become a feature of almost all team projects. It's become so popular, in fact, that some of its limitations tend to be overlooked. The first, and most obvious limitation is that all people must be in the same room. With the Net, that's simply not the case. People from different shifts or different parts of the country can participate in a brainstorming exercise as easily as the people just down the hall.

Another limitation of classical brainstorming is that people in the room who have senior organizational positions tend to have a powerful influence over the ideas presented. Research conducted at Carnegie Mellon University now indicates that these "rank queue effects" tend to disappear in online brainstorming. In other words, having the boss participate in a brainstorming session doesn't warp the process nearly as much as when folks are face-to-face in a single room.

Another limitation of classical brainstorming is that folks who are highly verbal and who reach decisions quickly tend to dominate face-to-face brainstorming groups. With online brainstorming people have time to formulate replies, and those who reach conclusions a bit more slowly can be on a more level playing field with their quicker or more verbal colleagues.

Finally, today's business teams are far more diverse than they were years ago. Certain groups are culturally conditioned not to shout out ideas in a public setting the way it is done in most classical face-to-face brainstorming. These people can participate quite easily and comfortably in the online version of brainstorming. You'll get access to perspectives and knowledge that would tend not to be available in traditional brainstorming situations.

We've spent a lot of time here talking about the value of the Net in enhancing team brainstorming, but the Net can enhance other team functions as well. The mailing list setup for virtual teams works quite well for ongoing discussion and long-term team development.

The authors consider it necessary, though, to have some sort of physical connection between project teams. We found that team members whose teams meet only virtually tend to take a longer time to become comfortable with one another than those who can also have face-to-face meetings.

We've also found, though, that teams who use an effective mix of face-to-face and virtual connection tend to reach somewhat more innovative suggestions and solutions than groups that meet only face-to-face.

There are some additional benefits to using mailing lists for virtual meetings. If team members are in widely scattered geographical locations or working different shifts, the communication that is established between team members will, in fact, also function as increased communication between those geographical sites or those time-separated units.

To some extent this exemplifies the "community-building" aspect of online communications that we've referred to. People who get to know one another, whether face-to-face or virtually via electronic communication, are far more likely to share information, consider what benefits others may bring to a project and know who to ask when a question or problem arises. Virtual teams can be a powerful way to help create a starting point for that kind of synergistic communication and community-building within the organization.

There's another way to put together a virtual team. That's to put all team members online at the same time. This can be done on the Internet or World Wide Web through several chat features, but right now it's most easily done on the commercial gateway America Online.

One of the strengths of the America Online service is the ability to set up virtual meeting rooms where people can interact in real time. One powerful advantage of the way this happens is that people's interaction can easily be captured and immediately shared, eliminating the necessity to have a great note-taker, who then needs to prepare minutes and distribute them.

All that's needed to set up a virtual meeting on America Online is a separate America Online account for each participant.

One of the authors has clients who use this technique regularly and maintain four or five America Online accounts simply for this purpose. A telephone call or e-mail determines who's going to use what account and when the meeting will happen. After that, it's a matter of folks' signing on and going to a previously agreed-upon private room. No special permission is needed and no additional fees are required.

At the production end of any business, one of the key challenges is sharing information well enough that all people related to the process understand what others are doing and can contribute their expertise and insight. The Net (and internal web sites, which we'll discuss in more detail in Chapter 10) provides many ways to enhance and enrich that communication process. As you face production and quality assurance problems and challenges, think about the different ways you can use the information resources on the Web or the Net, combined with the resources you already have internally to improve your production and the quality of product that you deliver to your customers.

Here's a tools/applications chart that illustrates some of the points we've made in this chapter:

Tools	Production & Quality Assurance Applications
E-mail	• Use e-mail to stay in touch with others in the production and QA efforts. • Transmit production information via e-mail. • Ask questions of equipment and supply manufacturers.
World Wide Web	• Check Web sites for the equipment and supplies you use often. • Check sites devoted to improved production and quality methods.
Autoresponders	• Use autoresponders to make quality standard information available.
Mailing Lists, Newsgroups and Forums	• Use mailing lists for virtual teams. • Keep up-to-date on key developments in your industry and production and QA techniques.

Chapter 8

Product Development

Key points

- Information and communication are at the core of the product development process.

- The Net and Web are ways to bring people responsible for product development into contact with customers and others on the front line.

- Use mailing lists and information gathering tools on Web sites to gather comments and suggestions that can become the ideas for new products.

- Three ways to keep track of the competition are to use clipping services, use databases and check Web sites.

- Surveys are a way to gather information online.

- Virtual product development teams can transcend the boundaries of time and geography.

- Use a mailing list to gather feedback during a beta test.

- Electronic communication can speed up the entire process of developing a new product and bringing it to market.

New products are the lifeblood of business. Improved products enhance profits. And profits are what make the product-development process essential in the rapidly changing, increasingly competitive business environment that we inhabit.

The Net, the Web and the technologies that support them provide an easy way to turbocharge your product development process. Using the techniques we'll describe below, you'll be able to pick up on new product ideas faster, develop products more rapidly and gather the feedback you need to bring them to market quickly.

As with many other functions online, information and communication are at the core of the product-development process. In most situations, virtual or otherwise, the product development process has five basic stages.

Stage 1. There's a *need* to develop new product ideas and test those ideas with other people within the organization and with potential customers and clients. Often this is done by special product development, or research and development, departments. In most businesses, there is some recognition that people on the front line have the best idea about what customers really want. But most businesses also fail to bring those ideas into play with the people who can actually develop the product.

Stage 2. Most businesses include research as a part of the product development process. This includes research into what competitors are doing as well as surveys and checks of available literature.

Stage 3. From research the process generally moves to development, where the core ideas are tried out, modified and turned into an actual product.

Stage 4. The next step is usually some form of product testing. Because of the influence of the software industry, we generally call this beta testing. Beta testing involves putting the product or service out in the marketplace and getting feedback from actual users about how well the thing actually works.

Stage 5. Once the product is fully developed, it's brought to market. From here the company considers issues of marketing and publicity, which we cover in Chapters 4, 5 and 6.

Let's take a look at this five-stage cycle in detail and consider how the Net and Web can enhance your product development.

Product ideas

Businesses traditionally had to rely on the people on the front line with customers to get customer feedback about what kinds of products or product enhancements might be most valuable. But with the Net or the Web, that feedback can come directly and quickly from customers themselves.

If you've set up a mailing list in which your customers and clients can participate by discussing your product and how they use it, you'll generate an unending stream of ideas for new products and enhancements to existing products.

In addition, the mailing list gives you a ready-made audience to test your ideas. It will be a starting point to search for people who might want to be beta testers a bit further down in the product development cycle.

If you have a company Web site, you can use a "question of the day" approach. Every now and then, ask customers to identify the biggest problem they currently face in business. The answers you get back can give you ideas about products or services that you haven't yet considered. Oh, sure, you'll get some ideas for products or services that just aren't within the scope of your business. But you'll also get several good ideas that you would not have thought of by doing traditional research.

Research

The sparking of ideas is just one part of the product-development research cycle. The research portion of most product development includes checking out what the competition is doing, scanning the available literature and conducting surveys and focus groups. All of these activities can be enhanced using the Net.

There are two quick ways to check out the competition. You can use a clipping service to keep yourself aware of what the competition is doing, and you can make checking competition Web sites part of your browsing activity.

With electronic clipping services, computer programs scan the newswires such as AP and UPI as well as the news release wires such as Bizwire for stories that meet criteria that a subscriber selects.

Those folders are then made available to the subscriber through a file or by e-mail.

You can use clipping services (which cost as little as $5 per month) to track media references to your competition or to competing products. For example, a clipping service that you set up to track a competitor will let you know about plant openings, new product releases, financial results and more.

You should also maintain a regular Web browsing discipline, visiting your competition's Web sites. Your Web browser will have a bookmarking feature (sometimes called a hot list or favorite places folder) where you can record the addresses of competition Web sites. Then, on a regular basis, check those Web sites to see what kinds of things your competition is talking about.

Next, you'll want to look at a search of the available literature. For this, online databases, most easily reached through CompuServe or specialized services, are usually the best bet. The database ABI/INFORM is a powerful general business database (available through several services) that indexes and abstracts articles from more than 1,000 business journals and magazines. There are also a number of specialized databases for particular industries and particular disciplines. A quick bibliographical search will supplement your other background research before you decide to move ahead.

In addition to the research we've already described, most companies are also interested in frontline research. One powerful tool for conducting frontline research is the focus group. A focus group, developed originally in the advertising business, is a group of people selected because they fit a particular profile, who are brought together to discuss an issue or to react to something.

Traditionally focus groups have been conducted in person. People are brought together in a room and asked to discuss an issue or their reactions to a particular product or service. The same activities can take place online. They can happen through the use of a mailing list or by bringing people together in a virtual meeting room. There are even companies springing up to carry out this function. They'll conduct virtual focus group meetings for you as well as the kind of focus group meetings you're used to.

Doing your focus groups online has the advantage of lowering costs and extending geographical reach. But there are a couple of downsides. For example, you get only people who are online. If you're looking for groups representative of the population as a whole, then an online focus group will not work.

Online focus groups will not work if you need to conduct the sessions around products that must be handled. If you're seeking reaction to a product, a traditional focus group will be more productive.

If you conduct customer surveys, you can supplement these with online surveys. There are two basic ways to do this. One way is to conduct a classic mail survey—only electronically. Use an electronic mailing list usually including people you've already identified as clients, customers or prospects. They may be people who have visited your Web site at some time in the past and requested a basic information file. They may have emerged through contacts made by your sales force. Whatever the source, these are people who fit the profile of those from whom you'd like to get opinions.

If you already have an electronic mailing list, reach those people with your survey by posting a comment to the mailing list stating that you are conducting a survey about a particular new kind of product. Ask people if they would like to participate. They can then respond by e-mail, and you can send them the survey the same way. An autoresponder is also a great way to conduct a survey automatically.

You can also conduct a survey on your Web site. If you do, you'll want to give people some incentive for completing the survey. An incentive can be as simple as a discount coupon or a special file of tips.

All of this research—the ongoing watching of competitor activities, the bibliographical search for new developments and the use of focus groups and surveys—can help you move through the research stage of your product-development cycle to development.

Development

Okay, now the preliminary research is done, and now you've got to come up with a product. Most of the time you'll put together a product-development team. We know from research that the best product-development teams are cross-disciplinary. Attempting to include clients or customers on the team has also become fashionable. You can do these things using the Net in addition to also actually bringing people together.

Because of the cost savings and effectiveness, you'll be tempted to use just virtual product development teams, but we'd caution against that. We found that you need real, physical meetings as a way of helping to establish community. The best research indicates that the best cross-disciplinary teams should use a mix of both physical and virtual meetings.

The Net can offer you a virtual product-development team as one way to carry out the development process. There seems to be two key ways to do this. In the first instance, the entire team is connected via a mailing list and brought together occasionally for real-time online meetings. We've discussed the details of this process in Chapter 7.

Another way to bring this about is to have a core team that is in constant touch via mailing lists and real-time meetings, supplemented by a group of experts, customers and others brought in from time to time to provide feedback. For example, the virtual product-development team might carry on the majority of business using its own mailing list and then use an expanded version of that mailing list to seek reaction from others. Or an expert opinion could be solicited and that expert opinion shared using the mailing list. Still another variation would be for the core project team to conduct its business using its own virtual meetings and mailing lists and to have periodic virtual meetings with an expanded team of experts and "reactors."

In addition to convenience, virtual product teams also increase the volume of communication and effectiveness. Studies by Lee Sproull and Sara Kiesler are clear about the qualitative advantages from using virtual teams for a variety of business tasks including product development. But you'll still need to pay attention to the same things you'd focus on with traditional teams.

You'll need to maintain the freshness of the team if your product extends for more than a year. You can do that by bringing new team members in and moving some of the older members off. Also, specifically for product development, as the cycle moves along, you are likely to need a different mix of skills. For example, you'll want people with production expertise at all points of the process, but you'll want stronger representation from this group as the cycle moves toward actual production. Once you've got the basic product together, then it's time for live testing.

Beta testing

When you're ready to test your product or service concept live, you must go out to the marketplace. That means finding people who are willing to participate in the test. If you already have a good mailing list and Web site set up, you probably have a good idea of some people willing to be beta testers for you. Their feedback can supplement the feedback you get from your product-development team and your field sales force and customer service contacts.

Once you've started the test, an electronic mailing list can be a great way of generating feedback quickly and easily. If your beta testers all have e-mail, putting them all on a feedback mailing list is a simple matter. Doing so will give them the chance to interact with each other and with the product team.

What if your beta testers don't have e-mail? Simply set up a low-cost e-mail account for them for the duration of the project. If they have a computer and a modem, set them up easily with an e-mail account using a local Internet-access provider and give them the software to participate in the test. Taking these steps may simultaneously introduce them to the joys of participating online and make them an ongoing part of your regular feedback system.

Bringing to market

This is the last stage of the classic product-development cycle and the place in which product-development begins to hook up with both production and marketing. At this point other communication tools come into play for sharing information between production/administration and marketing/sales.

The major advantage of using the Net as part of your product-development process is enhanced quality and speed. At the core of any product-development process is a need for the sharing of information, insight, and feedback. The Net makes all of these possible but speeds them up dramatically and therefore makes your product-development process more effective.

Here's a tools/applications chart that illustrates some of the points we've made in this chapter:

Tools	Product Development Applications
E-mail	• Communicate with virtual teams and with others important to the product-development effort. • Use electronic communication to speed up your product-development process.
World Wide Web	• Gather reactions on your Web site from users of your product or service. • Track competition by monitoring competitors' Web sites.
Autoresponders	• Provide a way for folks with only e-mail to retrieve information automatically.
Mailing Lists, Newsgroups and Forums	• Set up feedback systems to generate ideas or test new products. • Set up virtual product-development teams.

Chapter 9

Distribution and Customer Service

Key points

- Traditional distribution activities can be enhanced by communications and EDI applications.

- Information products can be distributed over the Net.

- The Net and Web can provide customers with support information whenever they need it while reducing the cost of delivering that information.

- Bulletin boards and Web sites are excellent ways to distribute corrections to software or information products.

- A first step for many companies is to make spec sheets, frequently-asked-question sheets and tip sheets available through a Web site or autoresponder.

- Hypertext linking can make customer support information even more effective and easier to use.

- Mailing lists can build a community of users, increasing their satisfaction with your products and their bond with your company.

We've said that any business function can be done or enhanced online—distribution and customer service are no exceptions. Companies around the world are using the power of network electronic communication to improve the way they deliver products and provide after-sales service to customers and clients.

Distribution

"Distribution" has traditionally referred to the function of getting goods from the factory to the end user. When the goods were physical objects, distribution was a purely physical function. In fact, the traditional function has been called "physical distribution" as well as "logistics." When distribution moves online, a clear distinction exists between the ways physical distribution is enhanced and the way distribution is done for information or other digital products.

Physical products

Physical distribution may seem to be entirely divorced from the online world, but that's not the case. True, you can't move a box of books or a machine part over the Internet. But to accomplish even traditional distributions processes, information must flow—and the faster the better.

In the last several years, one of the major movements in American industry has been the movement toward electronic data interchange. Electronic data interchange (or EDI as it's usually abbreviated) has been the way companies have achieved dramatic savings while at the same time smoothing out their operations. So what is EDI?

The principle of EDI is essentially this. Information relative to a shipment is entered once in a standard format. That information can relate to a number of things. It can be a description of the products in the shipment. It might be information on the route and transportation services to be used. It might also be information about the consignee, payments, billing, etc. In fact, almost anything that relates to the information that moves with a shipment can be put into a standard format and sent.

Now there's obviously a huge benefit from this. If all this information is keyed only once at the initiation point, all that must be added at points down the line is information generated at those points. This process replaces an old, frustrating process in which information would be rekeyed at each point. With EDI, the entire flow from the acquisition and purchase of raw materials through the production process to distribution to the end user can be integrated in a seamless format.

EDI has become so dominant in American industry that many large companies and retailers refuse to do business with people who are not participating in the program. Even small suppliers who want to do business with companies like Wal-Mart or certain defense contractors have loaded up their EDI wagon so they can get the business they seek.

But lots of companies have not yet seen the need for EDI. These companies can use the Internet as a way to enhance their distribution services.

The most obvious way to do this is through electronic mail. With electronic mail, basic information can be sent from one place to another at pretty much the speed of an electron. In addition, files can be attached to electronic mail so that standard documents can be moved from place to place electronically rather than needing to be retyped at each stage.

For example, a simple word-processing file that lays out a shipping document or invoice can easily be sent around the world attached to e-mail. A data file with product specifications can be sent with an e-mail from one place to another. The recipient can then merge data from the file with another application (such as production planning) without having to rekey the data. Using the information superhighway to transfer documents can improve ease and profitability for both you and the recipient.

But the advantages are even more dramatic when we start thinking about information products.

Information products

Products in digital form, such as books, spreadsheet files, computer programs and help files, can be distributed directly using the information superhighway. One of the authors of this book publishes an electronic newsletter, *Cyberpower Alert!*, about doing business online. It is published only electronically; there is no print version.

Electronic printing offers astounding cost savings when it comes to distribution. Starting a traditional print newsletter generally means charging a fairly high price and soliciting a low number of subscriptions because of the time and effort necessary to get and retain newsletter subscribers. Getting subscribers normally involves sending out extensive mailings at great expense to a wide range of people—very few of whom become newsletter subscribers.

In the digital world, the marginal cost of adding a subscriber is next to nothing. Sending two—or a hundred—newsletters costs virtually no more than sending one. Your profitability can start very early. Using electronic distribution makes it possible to bring down overall subscription costs and go for a wider circulation.

Subscription and distribution can be handled either automatically or with varying degrees of manual control. That's because listserv software gives you a number of options. You might set up your process so that subscription is automatic and a new subscriber is both added to the mailing list and billed automatically by a software program. On the other hand, you might decide to have the addition to the mailing list made automatically but handle the billing manually.

There are some other applications of this same kind of principle that look at the other end of the distribution channel for information products.

aBCD printing in Seattle, Wash., is a specialist printer of beta manuals (for the Beta-test version of new software). This company is using the information highway to handle the front-end of its distribution process. For a printer, that means the way it gets information. A client company with a beta manual it wants printed can send its information files to aBCD printing over the Internet. Once they're received, aBCD printing, using digital presses, prints an approval copy in a matter of hours. The approval copy is on its way via next-day air for client approval. Once the client makes any changes to and approves the document, the final version is printed.

Look at what's happened here. On the front end, the acquisition end, of the distribution chain, aBCD printing has cut the time, the expense and the effort other companies might put into obtaining material in physical form and then rekeying it into digital form. In addition, the electronic transmission has saved time and costs compared with sending a computer disk either through the mail or through a courier service. The reduced time, expense and effort give aBCD a tremendous competitive advantage.

At the end of the distribution chain, information products such as special reports can be delivered electronically. A consulting firm specializing in investment reports, for example, can have the report developed, prepared and e-mailed to a purchaser as soon as payment is received. If payment is also handled in digital form, this could be a matter of minutes. In a highly-competitive business such as investments, the ability to act in seconds can be an extreme competitive advantage.

Another area in which the digital distribution of an actual product has become popular is the software business. Recently we've seen several companies distributing their software online. This distribution happens in one of several ways. Some companies take orders, online and via phone or mail; then they "ship" the software over the Internet. Other companies allow a potential customer to download a version of the software. The software downloaded can be a full-featured version in encrypted form. In that case, once payment is received, the seller sends the buyer the ability to "unlock" the program, also via e-mail. The buyer can then use the program.

Many software companies are also allowing users to download demo versions of software users can try; they can then order the final version later. And there's always at least one more variant. We're now seeing "time bombed" versions of software that people can download. Those choosing to do so are allowed to use the software for a limited time, usually three or four weeks. At the end of that time, the full featured version becomes unusable.

All of these are ways to distribute software over the Net. But the possibilities don't end with software. In 1995 we saw rock groups distributing songs from their new CD releases over the Net. We'll see more of this in the future as the technology makes transmitting larger files across the Net easier and cheaper.

Customer service

Traditionally in American business, customer service has dealt with activities that happen after the sale of a product or service and that help the customer or client achieve satisfaction:

- Helping customers to use products or services.
- Solving problems people have using a product or service.
- Handling returns and credits.

All of these activities can be enhanced or actually done on the Net. Since all of the functions of customer service other than the shipping of a returned product are, in fact, exchanges of information, companies around the globe are finding ways to deliver customer service powerfully and speedily utilizing the Internet and the World Wide Web.

The Plastics Division of General Electric is a good example. It uses its Web site (http://www.ge.com/gep/home.page.html) to make huge amounts of technical information available to its customers. The customers, in turn, can get to that information when they need it—at any hour of the day or night.

There are an array of tools used for customer service on the information highway. Some of these have been around for quite a while, and others are just emerging as power tools for the information age.

Probably the oldest method of using the information highway for customer service was for a company to set up a bulletin board that users of its product or service could use to gather technical information when they needed it. The computer industry led the way here. For years, hardware and software manufacturers have maintained bulletin board systems to provide information to users of their products.

Normally these have worked with a single, regular telephone-line connection to a computer bulletin board. A person with a question about how to use a piece of equipment or install a piece of software would use communications software and a modem to make a call (often long distance) to the bulletin board. The customer would then be presented with an array of different options to meet his or her particular need.

A bulletin board might be devoted to any number of different classifications. For example, there might be a bulletin board for a specific software product. Or, you could set up a bulletin board for a particular type of use, such as product engineers.

The computer folks also found that bulletin boards were an excellent way to distribute fixes. A manufacturer might come out with a new brand of software, and only after it was out on the market for a while would they discover certain problems (bugs) in the product. Engineers would design software to correct the bugs, and a fix (or patch) could be prepared that was then placed on the bulletin board. Customers having the particular problem for which a fix was available could dial the bulletin board, download the fix and modify their own versions of the software.

To some extent this was "bag-your-own groceries" customer service. Users of support bulletin boards gained a certain amount of flexibility. They could call any time of the day or night. They could wander around the bulletin board finding topics of interest to them or clarifying their understanding of how the software functioned. The tradeoff for easy access to this information was that they had to find and use the information on their own.

When commercial gateways became popular, computer manufacturers began to use these to set up forums devoted to customer service for the manufacturers' hardware or software. The forums function very much like the bulletin boards, except the forums seem to foster a lot more dialog among users about particular products. With forums, the traditional bulletin board assess to fixes now also includes lots of ideas about applications, modifications, etc. In addition, forums usually have libraries of software additions, fixes and patches—all that can be downloaded.

In a sense bulletin board systems were the forerunners of customer service on the Internet. Forums, especially on CompuServe, are the next generation. Today, virtually any major hardware or software manufacturer in the computer business has a way of providing customer service through a bulletin board or a forum on a major online service.

If your company offers another kind of product or service, look to what has been done in the computer industry to find models for ways you could provide online service. Here are some of the things computer companies have provided by means of a bulletin board, forum or other computerized information source:

- Files of fixes, patches and additions.
- Information from users about applications.
- Product specifications.
- Answers to specific questions.
- Lists of frequently-asked questions.

All of these are aspects of customer service that transfer easily into a digital environment. The techniques were first developed on dial-up bulletin boards and then in the forums on commercial gateways. They're now being extended to newsgroups, Web sites and other Internet and World Wide Web applications. In addition, manufacturers of other products and even service firms can use the same service models that were originally developed in the computer industry, and use those models on the Internet and World Wide Web.

Now other types of manufacturers and service firms can use computer industry models—and extend the use of those models with a move toward the World Wide Web.

One way that lots of industrial manufacturers provide customer service using the Net is to make specification sheets easily available. Firms like Hewlett Packard Medical Instruments, Millipore and Ingersoll Rand Pump provide mountains of technical information. Those specification sheets are available to help two groups of people. Perspective buyers of their products can view detailed technical specifications that will help them make their buying decisions. Users of the products will use the information to help with maintenance of product application.

Using the Net to provide such information works because these companies can provide the information easily and inexpensively. The information is generally already gathered and often well-written. In fact, the first step many companies make when moving their customer service online is to gather already-prepared specification sheets, along with frequently-asked-questions lists and suggestions, and put them on the Web or on an autoresponder.

These can be set up as an array of autoresponder files or on a Web site with different pages for different specification sheets, for example.

The next step in this process for many companies is to use the linking character of the World Wide Web to make specification sheets even more effective. In effect, what these companies are doing is developing a help file similar to the help files in Mac and Windows programs. In those files, hypertext is used to provide a user with additional information about a word, phrase or function. On the Web the same technology can be used in precisely the same way. Spec sheets can cross-reference one another with the cross-references serving as links to take the reader immediately to a new area of interest.

By making customer service information available both on the Web and via autoresponders, companies make sure that their information is accessible to the broadest possible array of customers: those on the Web and those who aren't.

As companies learn more about doing business on the Net, they're developing specific applications that use old tools in new and powerful ways. One of the old tools that's being used in an exciting new way is the Internet mailing list or listserv.

For years folks have used mailing lists to gather information and keep up on a professional field. Information systems specialists using a particular piece of software, for example, have used mailing lists to keep up with the technical details about the particular product.

While technical specialists in computer products and services have used mailing lists and newsgroups for years to keep up on product information, regular business users have not. But increasingly we're seeing mailing lists devoted to different products that help noncomputer specialists keep up on the uses and fixes for particular products.

For example, a manufacturer of an industrial pump can use a combination of a Web site notice and an electronic mailing list to alert users of the pump to a change in maintenance specifications. That same manufacturer can use an electronic mailing list as a discussion that will identify strengths and weaknesses in the product and point out new and more effective applications developed by users themselves.

Mailing lists are also becoming a powerful way to build a community of users and friends around a particular product or service. It works this way. Your company has a product that lots of people use. You set up a mailing list to discuss the use of that product. People might suggest new applications. Others might point out problems that they've had, asking others, including you, for suggestions about how they should deal with the problem.

Then a funny thing starts to happen. If the folks from the manufacturer are on their toes, they pick up lots of good tips and early warnings about problems. Those ideas can form the basis for new product-development, which we covered in Chapter 8.

These folks can also use the mailing list as a convenient way to get information out to solve problems everybody seems to have. The mailing list gives the company a way to establish its own kind of presence. As that presence is established, a community is created. This happens because communities are built on a lot of interactions, whether the interactions happen face-to-face or over the Internet. With Internet mailing lists, loyalty and commitment to a particular product or service are built by the very act of learning to use it more effectively and sharing both its strengths and its weaknesses. As we move toward the 21st century, this may be one of the premier uses of global computer Network technology: building communities through repeated and meaningful interaction.

Mailing lists, newsgroups and forums are all methods to help build community. But sometimes no automated system is enough. Sometimes folks really want to check in with an honest-to-goodness living person. So some companies are now experimenting with what's called "virtual presence."

Virtual presence provides someone visiting a Web site the option to interact in real time with a real person. He or she might click on a button that says something like "Let me chat with a real person" and be shifted into a chat room where a customer service person is available. What happens then is very much like what has happened on America Online for several years with its Tech Live feature. With Tech Live, technicians answer users' questions in real time. This has started to happen on standard business Web sites as well.

Now there are three things to consider before you jump right into the virtual-presence bandwagon. First, ask yourself whether you really need virtual presence. If you're not aware of a significant number of situations in which people actually need one-to-one interaction, virtual presence may not be a good idea. Second, remember that virtual presence means staffing 24 hours a day—since the Internet is a global marketplace—or be very clear about the hours during which you will not provide service.

Third, consider that you will need adequate expertise in your virtual presence function to answer most of the questions people ask. Your credibility dips dramatically if when someone asks a question, they receive, "Well I'm not really an expert on that; let me get someone else." This situation gets even worse if your representative can't get someone else (in real time) and instead has to have someone else call that customer back.

As we've mentioned elsewhere, one of the critical trends in American business that the Net and Web are helping to foster is the move toward understanding precise marketplace niches. Engineers have different needs than do human resource people. People in the petroleum business have different questions than people in the retail food business. The Net and Web give you the ability to be highly specialized in the types of questions you entertain and the types of advice you give.

There's a clear trend toward being more niche-oriented in marketing, product development and other areas of business. The Web can help you become more niche-oriented. Because providing information in various forums is easy, you can offer specific types of product tips and suggestions for different groups of people. Because setting up a mailing list is easy and inexpensive, you can set up several for specific groups of people.

We can't leave a discussion of customer service without talking about the link to product development. Many companies have found that the best ideas for product development come from listening intently to their existing customers. Well, a mailing list is a great way to do this. Monitoring the mailing list can give you answers to questions about what kinds of features people really want. If you consistently see a question that begins with the words, "Does anyone know how to...," you've probably got a lead on a feature or even a new product that lots of people are interested in.

You can then use your mailing list as a way to continue your product-development cycle by refining your understanding of what people like or by doing miniature surveys.

Finally, your mailing list, newsgroup or Web site can also be a great way to reinforce your relationship with users and clients in other ways. You can offer specific contests just for people already your clients or customers. You can offer special benefits as well. And if you use your Web site, mailing list, newsgroup or forum as a way to do these things, you'll increase interaction with them and increase the active community built around your company.

Here's a tools/applications chart that illustrates some of the points we've made in this chapter:

Tools	Distribution & Customer Service Applications
E-mail	• Streamline distribution operations. • Distribute information products.
World Wide Web	• Provide support information. • Allow folks to check on order status. • Automate support operations.
Autoresponders	• Provide support information. • Automate some support operations.
Mailing Lists, Newsgroups and Forums	• Build a community of customers, prospects and friends who can discuss your product or service, sharing tips and ideas on application. • Keep up with key developments in your industry and in distribution and customer service.

Chapter 10

Administration and Finance

Key points

- In most businesses, administration supports everything else.
- By linking electronic mail with the Internet, you can connect parts of a business across vast geography and time differences.
- E-mail can be a powerful tool for increasing leadership contact with people at all levels of the organization.
- Internal Web sites can keep folks informed and connected and provide information for specific, occasional needs.
- Investor relations can be enhanced by putting basic information (like the annual report and financial statistics) on the Web.
- Savvy purchasing agents are using the World Wide Web and the Net increasingly to find information; they're using e-mail to carry on negotiations, ask questions and receive answers.
- The Web can help you cast a wide recruiting net, especially for highly-specialized positions.

In most business, administration supports everything else. And the Internet can be one of the key ways that that support happens and becomes more effective.

Basic communication

Many companies have already discovered the power that electronic mail lends to internal communication. But by linking internal electronic mail with the Internet, they can also connect parts of their business across vast geographic areas and many time zones. In addition, they can use electronic mail to link parts of the organization that would not normally communicate with one another simply because of when those employees work.

Some years ago one of the authors was working with a government agency that worked around the clock. The project on which he was working called for getting ideas from everyone in the agency about some organizational changes. Traditionally the folks who'd worked at night, the graveyard shift, had not participated much in that kind of idea generation. Naturally, most of the work was done during the day when regular administrators were present. If someone on the graveyard shift wanted to have real participation, he or she usually had to come in at a time other than their regular work time. Day-shift workers, by contrast, just quit doing what they were doing for a while and went to a meeting or a brainstorming session.

The system set up used e-mail to gather input and feedback. The results were striking. For the first time in the organization's history, people from all "times" of the organization participated. Even more importantly, when the changes were later implemented, a survey of people in the agency showed that satisfaction with the changes and with the process was high across the board; in previous similar projects, folks working the night shift had felt excluded.

Leadership by e-mailing around

As we rocket toward the 21st century, one of the key skills leaders will have to master is using electronic communication and the Net as part of their communications strategy.

We've got pretty good evidence, based on research done by Lee Sproull & Sara Kiesler, that organizations that use computer-mediated communication tend to become flatter than organizations that do not. Computer-mediated communication is a term that is used to describe communication technology such as electronic mail, distribution lists, bulletin boards and computer conferences where the computer is a direct medium of delivering the communication. We're also beginning to learn that people who actively use electronic communication and information media such as e-mail, newsgroups, mailing lists, etc., tend to be better informed and more proactive than people who don't.

Put those two findings together, and you have an organization that must be led in different ways than were the old stove pipe organizations, in which messages traveled up the pipe, across to another pipe and down to a comparable level.

Leaders in networked organizations will need to master the communication skills that go with changed and more complex paths for messages. More and more, their communication with people at all levels will be a routine, rather than rare, occurrence. More and more electronic communication, especially e-mail, will give people direct access to people at the highest levels of the organization. And, more and more, people at the "bottom" of the organization will have expert knowledge that the organization needs and needs them to share.

If you're a leader in a networked organization, you need to work hard at using the power of the communication technology to communicate with your people everywhere. Doing so is not hard, but it does take attention and effort.

Internal Web sites

One of the more interesting developments in recent years has been the development of internal Web sites by organizations. Organizations are taking the same technology used on the World Wide Web, Hyperlink, and using it to provide information to their own people on a variety of topics. Internal Web pages can tell members of the organization about people in other parts of the country and what those other parts do.

Internal Web pages can provide information on employee benefits, new strategic initiatives and any other information that should be shared across the enterprise. Many organizations are also using internal Web pages as a special kind of company newsletter. Web pages can use pictures and sound to give folks a real sense of who their colleagues might be.

One large corporation, for example, maintains their paper news-letter. But they've added another, internal Web, version as well. The internal Web version of the newsletter might include a picture of people mentioned in the paper version as well as a link to a page about that person telling who they are, what they're interested in, what their history has been with the company and so forth.

Other companies are using internal Web sites as ways to publish specialized information. Sales engineers, for example, might share information about their successes. A large company with many different sites might include separate pages for each site on the internal Web. In that way, someone traveling to a site they don't know well would have access to a site map, pictures of the building and recommendations about local points of interest.

If you're responsible for promoting significant events within your organization, consider putting up simple Web sites and allowing people and parts of the organization to post their own pages so that that information is readily available. The old saying, "Familiarity breeds contempt," doesn't hold here. In the case of an organization, familiarity breeds knowledge of what people do and bring to the enterprise and makes people more likely to be cooperative and creative.

Investor relations

Obviously, not all administrative processes are purely internal. In fact, especially for publicly-held companies, some of the most important communication happens with the real owners of the company: investors.

With more and more sophisticated investors out there on the Internet and World Wide Web, consider handling some of your investor-relations activities there. Many companies put their basic financial and annual reports on the Web. In addition to this, you can combine that function with easy e-mail response. You can encourage investors and potential investors to ask questions. Those e-mail responses can be routed internally to the folks responsible for investor relations.

Investor relations are important all the time, but they get more important when takeover activity is afoot. At times like that, the Web can provide instant information for the community and employees that will be affected. This has the additional public relations benefit of helping people from all perspectives understand the situation and how it's being handled. An example might illustrate things a bit better.

The IBM Corporation began a move to take over the Lotus Development Corporation. This was what financial folks call a "hostile takeover." In this case "hostile takeover" didn't necessarily imply there was nasty intent but did imply the takeover was IBM's idea, not Lotus'.

Two groups of people had a vested interest in the takeover activity and in IBM's plans were it able to acquire Lotus. First among these were the employees of Lotus. Within hours of the formal announcement of the takeover, IBM had a Web site up with information about the takeover and IBM's plans. The first day the site was in place, the vast majority of visitors were people at Lotus Development Corporation trying to find out what IBM might have in mind.

The Web site was an especially important information-sharing tool because U.S. Securities laws forbade the IBM Corporation from sending information to employees. Having information they can come and get was perfectly okay, but sending it was forbidden. By having a Web site, IBM was able to provide information to clarify its intent and its vision of Lotus and IBM working together. IBM was also able to help Lotus employees understand those same issues and make judgments about how they might be affected.

Once the original rush of employee interest was over, the next largest group that came to the Web site was the investment community. Analysts, brokers and others trying to figure out how this takeover would affect values, stock prices and the two companies came looking for information. The Web site proved to be an incredibly effective way to share such information with a broad range of effected individuals. Internet connections, e-mail and especially Web sites can be powerful ways for a company to share its story with its employees and with the investment community. In fact, various studies indicate that when a company puts up a Web site, the majority of the first visitors to that site are people within the company itself.

Some companies increase interest and get information and feedback from employees prior to taking the site live. Tom Vassos, of the IBM Corporation, for example, told us that his practice is to have new IBM pages and sites up on the company's internal Web for a week or so prior to going live on the Internet to get feedback and critique from internal folks. This has the added advantage of alerting IBM employees to issues their customers and prospects may ask them about.

Procurement

It goes by lots of names. Some people call it "procurement," others, "purchasing," still others, "materials acquisition." Whatever you call it, procurement is important to any business that makes a physical product. The materials you use, whether raw materials or goods already finished at some level, are vital to a high-quality finished product.

Other things that you buy are also crucial. The quality of the equipment your people use and the quality of the services brought through the purchasing department that others will use later are equally important and equally strategically valuable.

Savvy purchasing agents are using the World Wide Web and the Net increasingly as part of their strategy for success. Increasingly, they're looking to Web sites for information and to e-mail to carry on negotiations, ask questions and receive answers.

A number of specialized Web sites are set up for purchasing agents. Probably the oldest of these is IndustryNet. This particular site is setting out to make the purchasing agent's job easier. IndustryNet (http://www.industry.net) acts as a digital go-between for buyers and sellers in industrial companies. It asks buyers to enter detailed descriptions of the products or services they are seeking and provides information about manufacturers or suppliers selling those products. In mid-1995 Don Jones, CEO of IndustryNet, estimated that the 150,000 buying members represented companies spending more than $125 billion a year on parts, equipment and services using the World Wide Web.

Recruitment

When one of the authors of this book needed to hire management trainees for a multinational corporation (back in the days when these things were done on paper and by hand), his company would place an ad in the Sunday edition of *The New York Times* and receive a stack of resumes.

Someone, usually in the personnel department, would sit down and sort them into three stacks. One stack would be for the immediate no's, the folks who got "Thank you, but you do not meet our requirements" letters. Another stack was for obviously-qualified folks, people who seemed to be folks we wanted to interview. Other employees would immediately set to work on that pile, contacting those people about coming in for a preliminary interview.

And, of course, there was that third pile. The third pile included the resumes that a clerk couldn't make a quick decision about. This pile would be passed on to a manager in the operational area to decide whether or not to call that person for an interview.

In recent years, that process has become highly automated. Resume-reading software has lightened the load for many a manager; and, even more recently, sites have sprung up around the World Wide Web devoted to helping folks find positions and companies recruit employees more effectively.

Probably the best known of these recruitment services is Career Mosaic, run by Bernard Hodes Advertising. This is one of the top recruitment advertisers in print media, and a move to the Net was logical. As company representatives point out, their costs for Web notices are dramatically less expensive than the cost of print ads. And they design the Web site to encourage job seekers to return frequently. They lure job hunters with articles to help with the job search and articles by and about many of the employers placing ads.

Companies are also getting into the act setting up Web pages to aid in their own recruitment. Or they're directing people interested in the company to check out their Web site for more information.

Savvy job hunters are already doing that. They've found that a well-designed Web site gives them a lot of information about a company. That's especially helpful if they're looking for a job with a company that isn't publicly held and, therefore, about which there is not a lot of public directory information.

If you're getting the idea that administration and finance are key areas for using the Net and the Web, that's a good idea to get. We'd like you to think of two primary points as you finish this chapter.

First, communication is at the core of the administration and finance functions in a business, but it's also at the core of other functions. The Net and the Web give us a powerful way to improve the reach and the quality of our communication across and even outside organizations. They also enable us to make the communication two-way in ways we could only imagine years ago.

Second, the Net, the Web and the communication tools that they offer us should be used in new and interesting ways to also improve our leadership strategies. As you think about ways your company can use the Net and the Web, think about them as leadership communications tools. Look for new and interesting ways you can use their power to improve the ways you connect with the people inside and outside your organization. Look for ways to blur the line between insiders and outsiders when it comes to communication, an effective strategy made easier by the Internet and the World Wide Web.

Here's a tools/applications chart that illustrates some of the points we've made in this chapter:

Tools	Administration & Finance Applications
E-mail	• Connect your business across differences in geography and time. • Stay in touch with folks you lead and manage.
World Wide Web	• Use to get your management message out. • Use an internal Web site to communicate and train. • Put investor relations information on the Web. • Place recruitment ads. • Use to gather information for purchasing decisions.
Autoresponders	• Make investor relations information available on your autoresponder.
Mailing Lists, Newsgroups and Forums	• Keep up-to-date on key developments in your industry and in administration and finance.

Chapter 11

What's Next with the Net and the Web?

Key points

- Moving lots of information across the Web will become easier.
- Programming tools, such as Java, will increase the ways people can use the Net and Web and will also be more available for building effective Web sites.
- Secure transaction standards will allow consumers to make online purchases, and consumers will become more comfortable with online buying.
- The major change you can look for is the increased networking of the world, which will call for changes in the ways we do business and practice leadership.

Up until now we've spent most of our time discussing practical tools and strategies—the things you can use right away. Let's shift focus now to discuss what's likely to happen in the future: what to expect, what to capitalize on and what to be wary of.

As we've said earlier, the current adoption of the Internet and the World Wide Web by both individuals and businesses is a very similar to the adoption of television in the early 1950s. You can expect this phenomenon to continue for several years. To give you an idea of where we might currently be on the adoption curve, let's compare television set purchases and participation on the Internet.

In 1950, only about 10 percent of American households had televisions. By 1953, that number had grown to close to 40 percent. Right now, American households participate in the Internet at a figure somewhat less than 20 percent. Business participation is probably a bit higher, but there are no reliable figures for that. A comparison of these percentages tells us that our Internet use is now in a situation similar to television use between 1950 and 1953. If this is correct, what's ahead?

The mass interest in the Internet and the Web is likely to increase. Even now, *USA Today* includes a "Cyber Happenings" column right there on the television listings page. Look for more of that in the future. You'll also see specific guides to home use of things on the Web.

You can probably count on some battles over standards on the Net in the years ahead. Just as with television, we'll have to fight out exactly whose standard will win, what's more popular and so forth.

Finally, count on individuals and businesses developing newer and better ways to use the Net and the Web. We're still pretty much in the stage of adapting earlier tools and strategies to this great new medium, but that will change.

What about the technology? There are some exciting things on the horizon you ought to be aware of.

Moving information across the Web will become easier. This has to happen because folks want to hear sounds, see video and use the Web as a truly multimedia tool. Right now they're limited by the amount of information that can slide down the information pipe from the original provider or producer to their homes or offices. That's going to change in several ways.

High-speed modems will become far more common. The price is already dropping on the 28.8 modems. And those modems will increasingly use compression to get higher real-transfer rates than their basic speed will allow. Data compression is pretty much what the term seems to imply. It's taking an amount of data and making it fit in a smaller space. When that happens, it can be transmitted more quickly and takes up less disk file space.

We'll also see people developing several different ways to improve information flow through the information pipe by making the pipe bigger. ISDN (Integrated Services Digital Network) is one way that's likely to happen.

Phone companies across the country are beginning to make ISDN available to homes and businesses everywhere. There are still some problems in achieving a good installation, and we're learning how to make all the bits of the installation, the phone connection, the software and the ISDN line itself, work. But it will only be a matter of time before we get those problems ironed out, and you can have a super-high-speed connection in your home or office for the cost of not much more than a conventional analog phone line.

One other scheme for making the information pipe bigger is the so-called "cable modem." This method would use the cable coming into a home or business that currently carries television signals to carry Internet/Web transmissions. The advantage of this is that a lot more information could flow easily because of the capacity of the cable. That would mean that audio and video would be much easier to use on Web sites. Of course, for that to happen, there would have to be lots more cable connections to homes and businesses around the country. Cable companies think that's a good idea.

There are lots of compression technologies being developed right now too. Software engineers and designers are learning ways to create good graphics in fairly small files so they'll download quickly. Companies like Real Audio are developing a technology that will send audio signals across the Net in virtually real time. Now it takes longer to download a high-quality audio clip than it does to listen to that clip.

The same thing will have to happen with video. There are too many people working on the problem of video compression to have it remained unsolved for too long. Count on the possibility of soon being able to use both audio and video clips as part of your effective Web site.

Another tool that's received quite a lot of attention lately is Java, a programming language developed by Sun Microsystems that uses applets to share information, animate sites and several other things. "Applets" are, essentially, miniature programs. The term applet is derived from "little application." They sit out on the Net or the Web, and you'll be able to access them and use them when you want to.

One possible application for these applets is that simple files such as word processing programs would be out on the Net where you can use them whenever you need to rather than having the software on your computer. Applets also provide a way to improve the quality of interactions and animation on many Web sites.

The last area that we really should discuss is the area of transaction security. Many people feel that the Net is an unsafe vehicle for commerce. That may not be true in reality, but the perception of consumers is what really matter. Count on three different ways for people to make secure transactions before very long.

First, we'll see some form of basic, secure server. With this kind of technology, people will enter a credit card number and it would immediately be encrypted and sent to its destination. Methods already exist to do this, but there's no common agreement on standards.

Second, expect some form of third-party verification of transactions. This is already being done by companies like First Virtual Holdings. In essence the service-provider enables the merchant to verify credit card numbers and the consumer to ensure that his or her number is not accessible to anyone else on the Internet.

Third, DigiCash and other companies are also developing systems of digital cash. "Digital cash" is a kind of computer currency not traceable to the user. It's a lot like cash. We'll need it for lots of small purchases on the Net in which a credit card or check-like transaction is inappropriate. DigiCash is already in business; they started up in October of 1995. Look for DigiCash and other companies to develop this digital cash technology.

These are all technological changes you can expect, but they're not really the big change you should be looking for. The major change that's coming out of the Internet and the World Wide Web is the dramatically increased networking of the world. Individuals and businesses are being linked together more and more without regard to geography or time zone.

We'll have a smaller business world but a longer business day through automated means. For the business leader, all technological advances point in one direction: the Net will become easier and easier to use by a larger number of people for a wider array of functions.

All this means that you'll need to be thinking about how you'll use the Net for your own leadership. You'll need to find ways to lead in a world that's networked where information is available to all. This is the most exciting aspect right now to all these technological advances. Ultimately, the Net and the Web will form the basis for how we get things done and how we transform vision into action. We'll discuss this more in Chapter 15.

Chapter 12

Transforming Your Vision Into Action Online

This chapter guides you through the process of taking the ideas we've discussed and building a master plan to implement them into practical action steps to produce your desired business results. We'll help you do this regardless of whether you are a one-person entrepreneurial enterprise, the leader of a division or department or the CEO and chairperson of a multibillion-dollar company.

We have intentionally stayed away from the technical aspects of the Internet and emphasized the practical business possibilities to stir your ideas for how to use the Internet to do things faster, less expensively and more productively. The Internet is no more than a technological tool, albeit a very powerful tool, that will enable any businessperson to maximize the potential of his or her commercial endeavors to serve the marketplace.

In our discussion of "Basic Techniques and Strategies" in Chapter 3, we advised you not to get overwhelmed with the technology. There are always people around who can help you with the technical issues. As a businessperson, you learn see how the Internet tools, techniques, sites and ideas apply to your overall business purpose. Your primary job is to see how these fit into your overall business strategy.

Once a businessperson's imagination is stirred and captures the possibilities, his or her drive for action and results will set a thing in motion. As you have moved through this book, your challenge has been to connect what you know about business and what you are learning about the exciting online world with the technologies, tools and places you can put those to work online. As the translator, the savvy businessperson standing between traditional business people on one side and technological people on the other side, you should now take the next step into the world of doing business on the Net. The next step in establishing your company's presence on the Web and/or the Internet is to build a Master Internet Implementation Action Plan.

Start by bringing together a cross-functional team of experts from inside and outside your organization. The members of this team will assist you by providing information on the more technical/operational aspects of setting up a Web business presence. They'll lend their insights and ideas to enrich your vision and help you define the tactical steps necessary for achieving the vision. These tactical steps are the goals and objectives of your Master Internet Implementation Action Plan.

Pulling this team together will achieve two things. First, you'll sidestep two of the biggest mistakes made by many businesses dazzled by the prospect of establishing a Web presence. Those mistakes are:

1. Rushing in without a well-organized master plan.

2. Trying to single-handedly set the process in motion without securing the buying and support of your business team.

Second, you will have started to build a well-thought-out plan to assure the success of your project and empower your organization to implement and monitor your plan.

Now let's look at the primary steps you include in your plan. After we have discussed the pertinent details of each step of the Master Internet Implementation Action Plan, we will discuss a team-driven process for the development, implementation and ongoing monitoring of your plan.

The Master Internet Implementation Action Plan

[1] Select and form your core Internet Task Force Team, which will be your core cross-functional team of experts to create your Master Internet Implementation Action Plan.

- Select key opinion-leaders and/or business visionaries.

- Select high-level decisionmakers with power to make things happen.

- Include a representative from all primary functional areas (for example, someone from the primary functional areas covered in this book: marketing, sales, advertising & PR, production & quality assurance, product development, distribution & customer service and administration & finance).

- Include both technical experts and financial experts on this team.

[2] Identify your organization's strategic focus (existing purpose or mission) and introduce your Internet Task Force Team to how you could use the Internet as a strategic and tactical tool to enhance your organization's ability to achieve its mission.

- What is your business?

- What do you want to use the Internet tools to achieve?

- What are the benefits and potential Return on Investment (ROI) to using the Internet tools?

- What online activities are your competitors involved in? (Possibly prepare a brief business proposal with a solid analysis of these activities, specific applications you envision for your organization and potential ROI and benefits you anticipate. Such a proposal would introduce the members of your Internet Task Force Team to the compelling reasons for participating in a project of this nature.)

[3] Assign "Internet Awareness Building" tasks. Have everyone on the Internet Task Force Team:

- Read and study key chapters in this book.
- Connect to the Web and browse, using the Netscape browser, to become familiar with the nature of the Internet technology.
- Research and study similar and competitive business sites online.
- Read Internet magazines, trade journals and periodicals for what's happening and what's working in the online world.
- Subscribe, attend and lurk in industry-related mailing lists, newsgroups and forums.

[4] Use your Internet Task Force Team to brainstorm, develop and define your Web/Internet presence vision, goals and objectives.

(You might consider accomplishing Steps 4 through 11 in a one- or two-day offsite retreat with a professional facilitator familiar with the Internet.)

[5] With your Internet Task Force Team, review and discuss the six key online business models elaborated on in Chapter 2.

[6] Work with your Internet Task Force Team to match your company's functional needs and activities (from marketing, sales, production and quality assurance, etc.) with the six primary tools covered in Chapter 3 and the Internet tool matrices at the ends of Chapters 4 through 10 for those functional areas.

[7] Consolidate the Internet Task Force Team's collective Action Notes taken at the end of each of the primary functional divisions or departments of your business covered in Chapters 4 through 10 of this book. These Action Notes are the ones taken by the members of your Internet Task Force Team after they read each chapter of this book.

[8] Brainstorm and develop a list of specific goals, online strategies and tools for each of the primary functional areas of your business.

[9] Determine what requirements and resources you'll need to achieve the vision, goals and objectives laid out in your Master Internet Implementation Action Plan:

- Technical requirements and resources (level of access, hardware, software programming, etc.).
- Financial requirements and resources.
- Personnel requirements and resources.
- Knowledge/expertise requirements and resources.

[10] Based on your findings in Step 9, conduct a current situation analysis with your Internet Task Force Team to establish what resources you have and what you'll need.

[11] Create your Master Internet Implementation Action Plan. This plan should include:

- Specific project implementation timeline and key milestone dates.
- Specific goals and action steps for each functional department or division.
- For the marketing area, an overall focus that includes market analysis (competition analysis, analysis of existing and potential market's products and customer base) and projected business revenues.
- Key roadblocks and challenges with recommended action plans.
- Cost analysis.

[12] Select personnel from your Internet Task Force Team to form the Internet Implementation Council. The Council's charge will be to implement and monitor the Master Internet Action Plan by:

- Holding a company-wide kickoff meeting.
- Recommending and selecting key personnel for specific implementation tasks.
- Pinpointing areas of the plan that need refinement.

- Establishing the main vehicles for communicating updates on the progress of the Master Internet Action Plan.

- Checking implementation effectiveness.

- Tracking results by conducting internal and external customer feedback surveys, monitoring e-mail usage, numbers of new customer sign-ups on your Web site and mentions in newsgroups and/or mailing lists and reporting any other success stories and bottom line results achieved by use of the Internet.

Note: Step 11 of the Master Internet Implementation Plan process will probably take at least three sub-steps to achieve:

1. If you have done Steps 4 through 11 in a offsite setting with your Internet Task Force Team you will end up with a fairly well-developed rough draft of the Action Plan.

2. Assign the specific goals of this plan to individual members of the Internet Task Force Team, charging them with forming small teams of their own to flesh out action plans to achieve the goals they've been assigned. Each of the action plans should include the following information:

   - Specific project implementation timeline and key milestone dates.

   - Specific goals and action steps for each functional department or division.

   - For the marketing area, an overall focus that includes market analysis (competition analysis, analysis of existing and potential market's products and customer base) and projected business revenues.

   - Key roadblocks and challenges with recommended action plans.

   - Cost analysis.

3. After the individual action plans have been developed, pull your small teams together at an all-day meeting to:
   - Review the key details each of the plans.
   - Iron out any potential cross-functional conflicts.

- Incorporate the feedback of team members not on the small team.
- Receive final approval to implement recommended actions.

Possible roadblocks

Now let's address three possible roadblocks to the successful realization of your vision of doing business on the Net. These are:

1. You are not a large business and don't have a large resource pool of expertise to draw on to build your project team.

2. You do not have the capital necessary to finance the entire Master Internet Implementation Action Plan.

3. You're not the ultimate boss in charge of making this kind of decision and allocating the needed financial and human resources to set your plan in motion.

Although we do not claim to have all the answers to these roadblocks, we would like to offer some potential solutions.

Roadblock 1: No large resource pool

In the case of the first road block, we suggest these solutions:

1. Adapt the steps in the project planning process to meet your time consideration needs.

2. Consider forming a strategic alliance with some like-minded business peers. When we set up The Expertise Center Web site, we formed a strategic alliance with a local Internet service-provider to save on the time and financial investment of purchasing and setting up a server with a dedicated high-speed, high-bandwidth T1 connection to the Net. We both won because the Internet service provider got a large account while we saved on our upfront startup investment capital.

3. Interview a number of local technology experts and business owners who have already established Web sites for their online business activities. This will enable you to more clearly define your specific technological requirements and operational needs. Then consider writing your requirements into a request for proposal that will enable you to shop competitively to outsource some of your human resource requirements.

Roadblock 2: Not enough capital

In the case of the second road block, consider these solutions.

1. Fully develop your Master Internet Implementation Action Plan, and then break up your plan into logical bit-size phases with an established implementation timeline. Breaking the plan into affordable chunks (phases) can help you get started.

2. Choose to focus in on one specific objective in developing your Master Internet Implementation Action Plan. This focus gives you the advantage of "testing the Internet waters" while simultaneously developing your knowledge of the possible Internet business applications for a minimum outlay of capital and time.

3. Consider what you can achieve by using an inexpensive commercial online provider as the forum for your Internet business activities.

Roadblock 3: You're not the decision-maker

Finally, in the case of the third road block, we recommend several actions steps.

1. "Test the waters" of key opinion leaders in your organization for their thoughts and receptivity.

2. Ask your boss to entertain a proposal on such a project.

3. Develop a well-thought-out proposal with a solid analysis of the kind of online activities your competition and peers are doing, some specific applications and solutions the Internet technology offers your business and a detailed report on the ROI and benefits you anticipate from developing and implementing a Master Internet Action Plan. Remember, your boss did not get to be the boss without being constantly on the lookout for potential profit-making and productivity-enhancing strategies. He or she will likely appreciate your forethought, and you will demonstrate a professional commitment to the organization.

Why should your organization develop a Web/Internet presence as we move into the 21st century? Here are a few compelling reasons.

Results! That's what today's executives are looking for—faster, more accurate, enduring results. Yet in a business environment in which the rules of the game and the market forces change constantly, results are harder than ever to achieve.

In the race for survival, business leaders must meet the challenges and needs of both their newly-empowered information employees and their ever-demanding customers.

In the last century, technology has extended the reach of human beings dramatically. Radio, television, automobiles, jet airplanes, phones, faxes have all made it possible for us to reach out farther beyond ourselves and the walls around us. Perhaps the most powerful technological innovation to extend human reach in power began as a government experiment in the 1960s. It began as the ARPAnet, a government network linking computers at a few research centers, and it grew into the worldwide phenomenon called the Internet, more than 20 million people connected to one another through their computers.

Those connections give people Cyberpower, the power of information and connection. Cyberpower provides information when they need it in forms that they can use. Cyberpower provides connections with people—people in every part of the globe and with every imaginable variation of interest, expertise and need. Cyberpower provides buying and selling opportunities to business.

Business is only just discovering the power of this tool that transforms organizations and relationships. Cyberpower is a great wave of change businesses are catching. And Cyberpower presents the opportunity for someone out there to become the next Henry Ford. This means that it presents the opportunity to become phenomenally successful in business; but Cyberpower also presents the opportunity to have your own encyclopedia entry—that is, to change history.

Many business leaders are frustrated because "old ways" do not work in the new business environment of the Information Revolution. Old-style business structure is based on paper flow, traditional jobs and traditional boundaries between the organization and the "outside." Old-style business structure is based on control from the top down and obedience from the bottom up because people at the top of the pyramid have more information than those at the bottom. It is based on the idea that marketing and sales are things that you do to others, rather than with them. And it worked. Until recently.

But now trends in the news make obvious the fact that we are standing on the crest of a wave that will revolutionize the way we do business forever. Everywhere you turn you see and hear the buzz and blur of articles on businesses' reengineering processes through information technology.

A big change is going on. And it's more than just a change in technology. It's more than the Internet. It's more than just new markets and ordering pizza from your computer. But there's almost no practical information about what all these changes really mean for business and how a business executive can profit from them.

We wrote this book to help fill the information void this technological change is creating in our increasingly-networked global marketplace. Our goal has been to assist the business professional who wants to know what profitable results can be produced and how to make use of this powerful strategic tool called the Internet.

Appendix 1

Glossary

AOL. America Online, a popular commercial gateway with an easy-to-use graphical interface.

Archie. A tool that maintains and allows users to search large databases of publicly available files that can be downloaded by anonymous FTP (see FTP).

Archive site. A site that saves files of information or software for users to retrieve via either FTP or e-mail.

ARPAnet. An experimental network established in the 1970s by ARPA (Advanced Research Projects Agency), where the theories and software on which the Internet is based were tested.

ASCII (American Standard Code for Information Interchange). In the context of a file, an ASCII file is one that contains only printable text characters—numbers, letters and standard punctuation—that is universally accepted by every software program. Sometimes referred to a "simple text."

Asynchronous. The transmission of information without reference to timing factors on the receiving end. Someone can type in a message and send it off, but the recipient doesn't have to be around to receive it—recipients can then read and respond when they want.

Autoresponder. A text file that is sent automatically back to someone who sends an e-mail message requesting it. People can then download the file to their computer if they choose. This file can contain such items as articles, information about you and your products/services, or whatever you want to make available for people to automatically retrieve via e-mail.

Bandwidth. The size of the data transmission pipeline. The higher the bandwidth, the faster the information can flow per unit of time. You'll often hear people complain that they "need more bandwidth."

Baud. A measure of modem speed equal to one signal per second. The higher the baud speed of your modem, the more information you can transmit per unit of time.

BBS (Bulletin Board System). A computer system that automatically answers the phone and allows users (sometimes called subscribers) to exchange messages, mail and (often) files.

Browser. A program that you need to read files created with Hypertext Markup Language (HTML). These are the files that make up the World Wide Web. Netscape is a popular browser.

Chat. A service that allows two or more people to have an electronic conversation, a "real time" online dialog over the Internet. Many commercial service providers such as AOL, CIS and Prodigy also offer this service (see IRC).

CIS (CompuServe Information Service). One of the oldest and largest commercial online services.

Client. A software application or computer that uses information or files provided by another application or machine called a server. Computer networks are made up of clients and servers. On the World Wide Web, your browser is a client application that uses files provided by World Wide Web server software running on a computer called a server. In this case, your computer would be the client computer.

Communications software. A software program that does the translating between you and your computer, and between your computer and another computer. It allows you dial-up electronic bulletin boards, online commercial services such as America Online or CompuServe and computers that allow you access to the Internet.

Compression. The process of squeezing data to eliminate redundancies and allows files to be stored in less disk space. Often files are archived and transmitted in a compressed format to save space and transmission time.

Cyberspace. Often used in reference to the "nowhere" universe of networked computers where things happen online. The term was first used in a science fiction novel called *Neuromancer*, by William Gibson.

Dial-up user. A person who accesses the Internet through a modem over a phone line. This can either mean the user connects to a computer that is on the Internet and uses its services to contact the Internet or by making a direct connection to the Internet and actually becoming and functioning as a computer on the Internet.

Domain name. A name that also functions as an address on the Internet. For example, Bock Information Group, Inc., has the domain name bockinfo.com. Many businesses want a domain name that reflects either their company name or what they do. Domain names are registered with INTERNIC, the body responsible for keeping track of them.

Domain Name System (DNS). The system that keeps track of the domain names and which computers they are on, and also routes mail from one computer to another.

Download. To retrieve a text or software file from another computer to your computer.

E-mail. An abbreviation for electronic mail, which is one of the most used functions of the Internet. It is essentially a messaging system that also incorporates a file transfer function when needed.

Emoticon. A set of text characters designed to communicate emotion, body language, intonation and physical presence while communicating over the Internet. Another term for "smiley," and created with various combinations of colons and paragraph symbols to represent different expressions. Following is an example of a smile: :-)

Emulation. The ability of one computer to behave like another by means of a software application or hardware feature, an "emulator" is used by an ISP in a Shell Account (see separate entry) to allow its remote computer to acknowledge a personal computer as one of its own terminals.

FAQ (Frequently Asked Questions). A list of frequently asked questions and their answers. Many USENET newsgroups, mailing lists and software tools for the Internet such as Archie, Gopher, WAIS and so on maintain these for their participants and users so that other participants won't have to spend so much time answering the same set of questions. Although FAQs can be very helpful if you are a newcomer to the Internet, it is always advisable that the seasoned pro check them to so as to not violate the social guidelines when participating in a newsgroup or mailing list.

Finger. A program that lets you determine if a specific user is currently online or which users are online at a specific site.

Firewall. A system that protects one network (such as your internal corporate network) from another, untrusted, network (such as the Internet). The firewall system consists of a combination of hardware and software that allows some traffic (trusted or safe traffic) to pass through while blocking other traffic (unsafe or untrusted).

Flame. An angry response or personal attack against someone with opposing views or who has violated Netiquette—usually to an e-mail message, a message posted on USENET newsgroup or in a mailing list. People who frequently write "flames" are known as "flamers."

Forum. A special interest group devoted to a single topic. Forums exist on many general-purpose gateways such as AOL or CompuServe.

Freenet. An organization to provide free Internet access to people in a certain area, it is a community based, volunteer-built network with access usually made through the public library.

Freeware. Software that you can distribute freely and use for free, but for which the author often retains the copyright.

FTP (File Transfer Protocol). A tool (software application) that enables you to transfer text or software files between computers located in different places.

Gateway. A computer system that transfers data between normally incompatible applications or networks such as CompuServe's or AOL's gateway to the Internet.

Gopher. A popular Internet tool (software program) created at the University of Minnesota that displays files and directories in conveniently accessed menus or lists.

Header. The top portion of an e-mail message, containing several lines describing the route or process the mail went through before it got to you. This information is irrelevant to the average Internet e-mail user.

Homepage. This term is actually used in three different ways: It may refer to the first page a visitor comes to on a Web site. Or it may refer to the most important page on a Web site. On corporate sites, both of these are often the page with basic corporate information. The term homepage is also used to refer to the first page your browser goes to when you start it up.

Host. The primary or controlling computer of a computer network. This is a server that provides files, programs and other resources that are used by the client computers that make up the network.

HTML (HyperText Markup Language). Mark-up language of WWW documents that tells WWW clients how to display a document's text, hyperlinks, graphics and attached media.

HTTP (HyperText Transfer Protocol). A protocol or language used by WWW servers and clients to transfer HTML documents.

Hypertext. Provides the ability to move from document to document whenever a word or concept is introduced. It links documents and graphics through selected words and images. Simply point your computer's mouse to the word or phrase that is underlined and/or colored, click the mouse button and another document pops up, giving more details about the specified subject.

IRC (Internet Relay Chat). A worldwide network of people talking to each other in real time over the Internet rather than in person. (See Chat.)

ISP (Internet Service Provider). The company or organization that provides connections to the Internet, usually based on a monthly and/or hourly fee, for the end user, commonly referred to as a "service provider."

Listserv. A program that automatically manages mailing lists. It responds to e-mail requests sent to a mailing list and distributes them to the members of that mailing list. This term is actually the name for one of the software programs that performs this function. You may also see references to listproc or majordomo, which are the other two popular programs, but only listserv is used as the generic name for the type of program.

Log Off. the process of closing communications with a computer.

Log On. to connect to an online service by dialing the service and entering your e-mail name and password.

Lurker. one who reads and "listens in" on discussions without participating or contributing to the discussion.

Mailing list. an automated message service where subscribers receive e-mail postings from other subscribers on a given topic.

Modem. a device that allows your computer to talk to another computer or the Internet via the phone lines.

Net. A short way of referring to the Internet.

Netiquette (Internet etiquette). A set of operating conventions and codes of behavior expected to follow while online.

Newbies. Individuals who are new to Internet practices and etiquette, sometimes referred to as Internet tourists.

Newsgroup. An automated message area, usually operated by USENET, in which subscribers post messages to the entire group on specific topics.

Node. A computer system that serves as a host on the Internet. A node is connected directly to the Internet.

Offline. Actions performed when you aren't actually connected to another computer.

Online. Actions performed when you are connected to another computer.

Password. The secret string of characters assigned to your individual login name on that particular system. It prevents others from easily accessing your computer accounts.

Post. To place a message on a bulletin board, in a forum or in a USENET newsgroup for public reading.

Protocol. The codes and procedures that make it possible for one computer to talk to another computer and exchange data.

Router. A computer system that makes decisions about which path Internet traffic will take to reach its destination.

Server. A computer that is configured to communicate with clients and provide access to the files stored on the server computer. A file server makes files available, a WAIS server makes full-text information available through WAIS protocol, a WWW server makes stored hypertext files available to the browser client.

Service provider. A company or other entity that provides Internet or other computer services available to a third party (see ISP).

Shareware. Software available on a trial at no costs from FTP sites. After the trial period, users are required to register and send in the registration fees, which entitle them to documentation, technical support and program upgrades.

Shell account. An account that allows dial-up users with standard communications software to access the Internet via the ISP's computer, which usually runs the UNIX operating system.

Signature file (.sig file). A file typically between four and eight lines long, that users append to the end of their electronic mail and USENET newsgroup or mailing list message postings. It's a good way to get a promotional message out about your business or yourself without offending Internet users with blatant advertisement. This is sometimes referred to as an "Electronic Business Card."

SLIP (Serial Line Internet Protocol). A protocol, like PPP, that lets a Macintosh computer pretend it is a full Internet machine using only a modem and a phone line.

Smiley. See emoticons.

Snail mail. The standard name on the Internet for paper mail because e-mail can travel across the world in seconds and paper mail takes days.

Spamming. The act of sending hundreds of inappropriate posting to USENET newsgroups and mailing lists. Old-time Internet users consider this to be a very serious breach of Netiquette.

Subject line. The line on the e-mail message that tells you what it's about.

Surf. A term for browsing through the Internet and going from computer to computer on the Internet, usually without staying too long.

Sysop. A person who monitors online conversations to be sure they stay on track and above board.

TCP/IP (Transmission Control Protocol/Internet Protocol). A special computer language to guarantee the safe arrival of data at its intended destination, this is the base protocol on which the Internet is founded.

Telnet. A software tool that enables you to log into a remote computer from the computer you are sitting at. It allows you to access and direct the remote computers to do such things as search the remote computers database.

Text file. A file that contains only characters from the ASCII character set, with no graphics or special symbols.

Thread. A series of messages or conversations that follow a single thought or topic.

UNIX. An operating system specializing in customizability and multi-user capabilities that it's in wide use on the computers on the Internet. It uses a rather cryptic language that can be very difficult for the average Internet user and thus the rise and popularity of "Point and click" software, which is much more user friendly.

Upload. To send a test or software application file from your computer to a remote computer on the Internet, a commercial online service or a bulletin board.

URL (Uniform Resource Locator). A standard addressing system used in the World Wide Web that can reference any type of Internet file, enabling a WWW client to access that file. It contains information about the method of access or protocol, the server computer to be accessed and the pathname of the file to be accessed.

USENET. A bulletin board network system, linked to the Internet, that houses the popular special interest newsgroups.

Veronica. A service, very much like Archie, that is built into Gopher. Just as Archie allows you to search all FTP sites for files, Veronica allows you to search all Gopher sites for menu items such as files, directories and other resources.

Virus. A software application designed to infect existing software and cause damage.

WAIS (Wide Area Information Servers). An efficient and user-friendly Internet indexing system that enables users to look up information in databases and libraries.

WWW (World Wide Web). An invisible network within the larger network of the Internet. It is a hypermedia exchange system that allows users to exchange linked text, images and sounds over the Internet.

ZMODEM. The fastest and most popular file transfer protocol.

Appendix 2

How to Build Your Company's Web Site

At several points in this book we've talked about building a Web site and designing it so that it's effective. In this appendix we're going to cover the basic steps you need to follow to accomplish that task.

1. Begin with a solid business objective

There's so much hype about the World Wide Web now that many companies are setting up Web sites simply because they think they should. To be most effective, have an idea of what you want to accomplish with your Web site and what business purpose it should serve.

Look at the six models that we outlined earlier for improving profits on the Web, and use these as a starting point for your statement of your Web business objective.

2. Design the site

Once you've decided on your objective, design a basic site. Consider four things: the tools available; models of sites you like; ways your customers, prospects and friends will come to you; and what your business is. You can address these in no particular order. In fact, very often people touch each of these bases more than once as they go through the process of site design.

When you're thinking about tools, pick tools that work with the strength of the medium. Consider Web links, mailing lists, forms, surveys, information-sharing methods and other things we've discussed in this book.

Spend some time looking at other sites to determine what kinds of things you like. That way you'll be able to direct a site designer to and help the designer get inside your head.

Design your site from the outside in. Ask yourself, "What do people look for when they come to us? What kinds of questions do they often ask us first on the telephone? What are the most common questions that prospects ask our sales people?"

As you answer each of these questions, consider what information is necessary to help your customer or client at that point and how you can help them move toward a decision to become involved with you.

Simultaneously, design your site from the inside out. Think about who you are, what you do and what your products and services are. What features do they have? What benefits do they provide?

Mind mapping can be an especially powerful tool for both of the above analysis functions. With mind mapping, you connect concepts and ideas on paper in the same way that you do in your head. Pick up a book such as Joyce Wycoff's *Mind Mapping* or Tony Buzan's *Making the Most of Your Mind* for details on using this thinking tool.

One particular piece of software can be very helpful at this point because it handles mind mapping. It also can give you a visual demonstration of links. That software is called "Inspiration." It's available for both Macs and PCs through the standard software channels.

If you do rigorous analysis on your site design, all of your analysis, tools, and models—inside/out and outside/in—will eventually come together to give you a clear idea of what your site will be. At this point, you should have a diagram of your site and its links.

3. Develop the site

Begin your site development by developing a mock site. A mock site is a Web site that you develop on your own computer, not on the

Net. Working on your computer lets you work out the information, links, proofreading and other issues before you take it live.

When you've developed a good site on your own computer, put it on the Web for a Beta test. At this point you won't go public with your site; you're just putting it out there to see how things work and buying some time to finish some other activities relative to your site announcement.

With your site out there on the Web, test it with a number of browsers. Be sure to include Netscape, browsers from the commercial gateways and several versions of Mosaic. Check out your site at various times of the day and night. Pay special attention to how fast things load, how easy things are to use and whether your links work effectively.

While you're testing the site, get ready for the real thing. Modify your printed materials so that your URL appears on your brochures, business cards, advertisements and any other materials. Get your employees up to speed, especially your customer service and sales folks who may get questions about the Web site.

And prepare your roll out plan. That includes registering your site with all of the appropriate search engines and making sure you know how you're going to introduce your new tool to your clients, prospects and friends.

4. Go public

Once your site and materials are ready, go public. Don't make this move until your printed materials are ready and people can find you using the Web's search utilities.

Issue a news release to your trade press about your new Web site, and send copies of that release to your entire customer and prospect base. Have your sales force use the new Web site as a reason to make a call. They can introduce the Web site by showing it to purchasing agents and others who might be interested in gathering information from it. Then have them ask purchasing agents to add your Web site to the purchasing agents' hot lists or bookmark files.

5. Update and improve your site

This is such a fast-changing and developing area of business that you're going to want to stay on top of things. Begin by checking out lots of sites as part of your daily routine. Have your other key executives do the same thing. When you find things you like, make notes and add them to your hot list files so you can show them later to the person responsible for your Web site.

Consider regular updates to your site and make sure that the most recent update date appears on the site itself.

Watch for times when you'll want to redesign the site. Many of our clients want to redesign the site after it's been up for three or four months. By then you, too, will have a clear idea of who's using your site, why and when.

These are the basic steps for setting up a Web site. Remember, though, that this is a project that is really never done. As long as you have a living business, your Web site will need to reflect that. And as long as it reflects your changing business, it will need to change to reflect your evolving business objectives and environment.

Appendix 3

Your Personal Executive Information Strategy

The Net and Web are powerful information tools, and they've altered the way that most executives can now keep up with important information. At the same time, they've multiplied the amount of information that's available. Here are some tips on putting together a personal information strategy, a strategy that will keep you on top of the information you need to use and still give you time for other things important in your life.

As you put your strategy together, you'll find that you need a mix of both key print media and digital media. Let's start with the print media.

Your basic information strategy should include regular reading of a daily newspaper. Most business folks find that a national newspaper such as *The Wall Street Journal* is an excellent place to start. Even though the *Journal* is setting up an online presence, the print version of the paper is one of the easiest papers to scan quickly for critical information.

Most folks also need a regular news magazine. There are the usual *Time*, *Newsweek*, and *U.S. News and World Report*, but many people find the *Economist* an excellent source of both good information and a worldwide perspective. The *Economist* has a World Wide Web site and will be adding material to it as well, so you can supplement your reading with additional digital information.

Finally, most people need to stay on top of their profession or industry. And, for most folks, that includes regular reading of one or more professional journals. Pick the one or two that are most important. That way you're sure to get the reading done. And you'll get the most important reading done, so don't worry about all of the other articles that you're missing. Focus on the most important stuff and make sure that's done first.

In addition to print media, be looking at ways to use digital media. You have two basic objectives: keeping up with information and tracking your competition. Do these by mixing a clipping service with a review of critical Web sites.

Clipping services are services that scan news wires and deliver articles to you based on a profile that you develop. There are essentially three kinds of clipping services.

First, services like Heads Up work on a fixed-category basis. For these you select from among several specific categories, and the service will deliver mail to your mailbox on a regular basis.

Second, other clipping services, such as the services available though the Executive Option on CompuServe, put your news stories in a folder based on key words you select. On a frequent basis, go to the folder, review the articles, download the ones you want and delete the rest.

Most of these services work using a Boolean search technique. That's the "and, or, not" kind of search you remember from your school days.

A third, newer kind of service is News Hound, a service of the *San Jose Mercury News*. News Hound uses a profile of key words you develop but searches using fuzzy logic. In that way, it's more likely to select stories with similar, but not exactly the same, words as you selected. Fuzzy logic is pretty much the technique human beings use to search, and this kind of search method for a computer shows a great deal of promise. News Hound delivers stories to your e-mail box rather than giving you a place to go for them.

Use clipping services to scan the news wires for mentions either of key words related to your industry or key competitors. Clipping services are quite inexpensive, sometimes as low as $5 a month. An especially good one is the News Hound Service. You can find out more about it by calling 1-800-818-NEWS.

You'll also want to scan key Web sites for information. Those Web sites can fall into any one of three categories: industry sites, competitor sites and information sites.

1. Industry sites are key informational sites related to your industry, business or profession. Associations often put these Web sites up. Associated Web sites devoted to a particular industry usually have a wealth of information about the topic. You can check these Web sites to keep abreast of changing industry trends and critical issues.

2. Track your competition easily by putting together a list of competitor Web sites and adding them to your bookmark or hot list file. Then once every couple of weeks, spend 15 or 20 minutes checking out those Web sites to see what the competition is up to. You might also want to check these Web sites if you pick up a hot news item from your clipping service mentioning tracking a competitor by name.

3. General information sites are the sites of major newspapers and magazines. You'll find some that offer exactly the sort of information you want to get. For example, you might not want to subscribe to the Economist magazine but might find it helpful to check the Economist Web site from time to time. Or you might find that *Business Week* is a magazine you don't get around to reading but can scan quickly in its online form.

Your information strategy should also include key newsgroups and mailing lists related to your professional interest. Here you'll find it possible to connect with colleagues around the globe. Ask questions, give answers and gain insight.

In addition to these parts of your regular daily or weekly scanning practice, also conduct searches using a bibliographic database about once a month. Conduct searches related to your key competitors and key industry issues. You might want to conduct an additional search on general business information. For these kinds of searches, we'd recommend using the database ABI/INFORM, which is available through the CompuServe Information Service. This database is also available on CD ROM, and many public and university libraries have it.

Once you've developed a basic search strategy, you can delegate the actual searching and the printing of information to others. One of the reasons we suggest the ABI/INFORM database is that it provides abstracts of key articles. You can scan these to determine whether or not you need or want to see full articles.

In this age of the rising tide of information, a strategy for handling information is almost essential. Make the Net and the Web a key part of how you stay on top of fast-breaking developments and sort through the clutter to find just the right information for your strategic purposes.

Index

Both Wally and Jeff are involved in helping organizations use the Net to improve their profitablity. They offer:

- consulting
- videotapes
- audiotapes
- and more...

For more about any of these or to have either Jeff or Wally speak to a group, contact information is as follows:

Jeff Senne
800-786-4421
jsenne@cyberpower.com

Wally Bock
800-648-2677
wbock@cyberpower.com

or...

check out the Cyberpower website for more at
http://www.cyberpower.com